Writing Effective E-Mail

Improving Your Electronic Communication

Revised Edition

Nancy Flynn and Tom Flynn

A Crisp Fifty-Minute™ *Series Book*

This Fifty-Minute™ book is designed to be "read with a pencil." It is an excellent workbook for self-study as well as classroom learning. All material is copyright-protected and cannot be duplicated without permission from the publisher. *Therefore, be sure to order a copy for every training participant by contacting:*

THOMSON
™
NETg

1-800-442-7477 • 25 Thomson Place, Boston MA • www.courseilt.com

Writing Effective E-Mail

Improving Your Electronic Communication

Revised Edition

Nancy Flynn and Tom Flynn

CREDITS:
Product Manager: **Debbie Woodbury**
Editor: **Ann Gosch**
Production Editor: **Genevieve McDermott**
Manufacturing: **Stephanie Porreca**
Production Artists: **Nicole Phillips, Rich Lehl, and Betty Hopkins**

For more information contact:

NETg
25 Thomson Place
Boston, MA 02210

Or find us on the Web at **www.courseilt.com**

For permission to use material from this text or product, submit a request online at www.thomsonrights.com.

Trademarks
Crisp Fifty-Minute Series is a trademark of NETg. Some of the product names and company names used in this book have been used for identification purposes only, and may be trademarks or registered trademarks of their respective manufacturers and sellers.

Disclaimer
NETg reserves the right to revise this publication and make changes from time to time in its content without notice.

ISBN 1-56052-681-5
Library of Congress Catalog Card Number 2003101619
Printed in the United States of America

6 7 8 9 10 08 07 06

Learning Objectives For:

WRITING EFFECTIVE E-MAIL

The objectives for *Writing Effective E-Mail, Revised Edition* are listed below. They have been developed to guide you the user the core issues covered in this book.

THE OBJECTIVES OF THIS BOOK ARE TO HELP THE USER:

1) Review workplace e-mail risks and learn strategies for writing safe and secure e-mail to keep the organization in business and out of court.

2) Explore the role clear and concise e-mail plays in positioning both employees and organizations before internal and external audiences.

3) Explore strategies for writing persuasive e-mail messages that are opened and acted upon—not ignored and deleted—by readers.

4) Learn technological tools and common-sense techniques to help senders and receivers successfully manage, organize, and transmit their e-mail.

ASSESSING PROGRESS

NETg has developed a Crisp Series **assessment** that covers the fundamental information presented in this book. A 25-item, multiple-choice and true/false questionnaire allows the reader to evaluate his or her comprehension of the subject matter. To download the assessment and answer key, go to www.courseilt.com and search on the book title, or call 1-800-442-7477.

Assessments should not be used in any employee selection process.

About the Authors

Nancy Flynn is founder and executive director of The ePolicy Institute™, an organization devoted to helping employers reduce electronic liabilities, while helping employees enhance their e-mail writing and e-mail management skills. Through the ePolicy Institute Speakers' Bureau, Ms. Flynn delivers keynote speeches and conducts e-mail writing, e-mail management, and e-policy seminars for corporations, associations, and government entities throughout North America and around the globe.

Recognized for her expertise in e-mail writing, e-mail management, and e-policy development, Ms. Flynn has been featured in *The Wall Street Journal, US News & World Report,* and *Woman's Day,* and on USAtoday.com, National Public Radio, and other national and international media outlets. In addition to *Writing Effective E-Mail,* Ms. Flynn is the author of several other books including The *ePolicy Handbook, The $100,000 Writer,* and Crisp Publications' *Networking for Success.* To book Ms. Flynn as a speaker or for more information on safe and effective e-mail, visit www.epolicyinstitute.com or e-mail nancy@epolicyinstitute.com.

Tom Flynn is senior information systems project leader for Liebert Global Services. He has been working with midrange, mainframe, and personal computer systems since 1982. He is fluent in numerous software development languages and has a wide range of experience with several varieties of e-mail software. Mr. Flynn's e-mail address is experts@epolicyinstitute.com.

Tom Flynn and Nancy Flynn are brother and sister.

Customized workshops and keynote speeches based on the material presented in this book are available from The ePolicy Institute. Please contact Ms. Flynn for information:

Nancy Flynn, Executive Director
The ePolicy Institute
2300 Walhaven Court, Suite 100A
Columbus, OH 43220

Phone: 614-451-3200 Fax: 614-451-8726
E-mail: nancy@epolicyinstitute.com
Web site: www.epolicyinstitute.com

Dedication

Nancy Flynn dedicates this book to her husband, Paul Schodorf, and their children, Bridget and Tim.

Tom Flynn dedicates this book to his loving wife, Sammi, and their son, Luke.

How to Use This Book

This *Fifty-Minute™ Series Book* is a unique, user-friendly product. As you read through the material, you will quickly experience the interactive nature of the book. There are numerous exercises, real-world case studies, and examples that invite your opinion, as well as checklists, tips, and concise summaries that reinforce your understanding of the concepts presented.

A Crisp Learning *Fifty-Minute™ Book* can be used in a variety of ways. Individual self-study is one of the most common. However, many organizations use *Fifty-Minute* books for pre-study before a classroom training session. Other organizations use the books as a part of a systemwide learning program—supported by video and other media based on the content in the books. Still others work with Crisp Learning to customize the material to meet their specific needs and reflect their culture. Regardless of how it is used, we hope you will join the more than 20 million satisfied learners worldwide who have completed a *Fifty-Minute Book*.

Contents

Part 4: Polishing Your Cybermanners

Part 5: Formatting Your E-Mail Message

Part 6: Managing E-Mail Overload

Appendix

Introduction

E-mail is the most common, convenient—and potentially costly and cumbersome—means of business communications. From customer service representatives and sales managers to administrative professionals and CEOs, nearly everyone uses e-mail to communicate with customers and colleagues. North American business has experienced a 66% increase in workplace e-mail in recent years, with 1.4 trillion messages sent in 2001, up from 40 billion in 1995, according to the research firm International Data Corp.[1]

With all that e-mail traffic, the potential for electronic disaster is huge if you are not careful to write messages that are as safe and secure as they are clean and clear. Among the workplace disasters e-mail can trigger:

> **Workplace lawsuits:** Includes claims filed by employees and outside parties offended by inappropriate messages flowing in and out of your organization's e-mail system. Also includes suits filed by employers against employees for criticizing, defaming, or harassing the organization online.

> **Lost productivity:** Time spent writing, reading, and replying to messages—business-related or not—is productive time lost, never to be recaptured.

> **Mishandled leads, lost sales, and customer service disasters:** A poorly worded, illogical, or inaccurate e-mail message can drive away customers and destroy sales. All business correspondence—electronic or hard copy—projects an image of you and your organization. In the battle for the reader's on-screen attention, carefully written, thoughtfully worded e-mail free from inappropriate language and mechanical errors is sure to come out on top.

> **Financial losses:** E-mail makes it easy for disenchanted employees, vengeful ex-employees, and thoughtless writers to steal proprietary data and send confidential company information to competitors. When leaked to the public, internal e-mail has been known to trigger a sharp decline in public-company stock prices.

> **Ruined reputations and other public relations nightmares:** Written in haste and sent without consideration of the consequences, inappropriate e-mail can lead to workplace lawsuits, employee terminations, media scrutiny, and public embarrassment.

The first edition of *Writing Effective E-Mail* focused primarily on composing, presenting, and managing e-mail, but this newly revised edition takes on the more comprehensive task of helping the reader avoid e-mail liabilities while creating electronic documents that are as persuasively and powerfully written as they are risk-free.

To that end, we offer the following e-mail self-assessment to help you gauge your understanding of electronic risks, evaluate your e-mail writing skills, and recognize opportunities to approach electronic communication in a more strategic way.

EVALUATE YOUR E-MAIL USAGE

1. Do you sometimes use your organization's e-mail system for personal use?   ❏ Yes   ❏ No

2. If the answer to question 1 is yes, to what extent and under what circumstances do you do so? _____

   _____

3. Does your organization have an e-mail policy?   ❏ Yes   ❏ No

4. On a typical workday, how many minutes do you spend reading and writing e-mail messages?

   ❏ 0-14 minutes   ❏ 15-29 minutes   ❏ 30-59 minutes   ❏ 60 or more

5. How many e-mail messages do you receive on a typical workday?

   ❏ 0   ❏ 1-11   ❏ 12-23   ❏ 24-49   ❏ 50-99   ❏ 100+

6. Have you ever written an e-mail message that unintentionally irritated, offended, or angered the reader?   ❏ Yes   ❏ No

7. Has your employer ever disciplined or terminated an employee for sending or receiving inappropriate or offensive e-mail?   ❏ Yes   ❏ No

8. Have you ever received an inappropriate e-mail message at work?

   ❏ Yes   ❏ No

9. If the answer to question 8 is yes, what type of message was it?

   ❏ Racist   ❏ Sexist   ❏ Obscene   ❏ Menacing   ❏ Other

10. E-mail can be used as evidence in workplace lawsuits.

    ❏ True   ❏ False

11. The best way to reduce e-mail risks is to control written content.

    ❏ True   ❏ False

Assessing Your Responses:
Where You Stand in Relation to Other E-Mail Users

The following information will tell how you, as an e-mail user, compare with others who are sending and receiving electronic messages in the workplace.

1. Although 86% of employees send and receive personal e-mail at work,[2] you may be violating your employer's e-mail policy if you do so. Do not risk disciplinary action or termination. Read, understand, and comply with your organization's e-mail policy.

2. Most employers take one of three approaches to personal e-mail: (1) all personal e-mail is banned; (2) a limited amount of personal e-mail is allowed, provided it falls within established guidelines; or (3) personal use is permitted, but only after normal business hours. Play it safe. Do not write personal e-mail messages until you know exactly where your employer stands on the issue.

3. According to a survey conducted by the American Management Association, *US News & World Report,* and The ePolicy Institute, 81% of employers have a written e-mail policy.[3] Chances are your employer has one too. If that is news to you, contact your human resources director or chief information officer and ask for a written copy of your organization's e-mail policy.

4. *The Wall Street Journal* reports the average office worker spends 49 minutes a day e-mailing, while top management spends about four hours a day sending, receiving, and reading e-mail.[4] How do you compare?

5. An effective e-mail management strategy can help save you from drowning in e-mail. E-mail management techniques for individuals and organizations are provided in Part 6 of this book.

6. E-mail is a cold medium. Without the benefit of intonation, facial expression, or body language, it is easy for e-mail writers to offend or irritate readers. Before clicking *Send,* objectively assess the message's tone and content. If the reader could misinterpret or be offended by your message, rewrite it.

7. More than 46% of U.S. employers have disciplined or terminated employees for e-mailing sexually suggestive or explicit material. Another 28% have disciplined or terminated employees for sending menacing, harassing, discriminatory, or otherwise objectionable e-mail. And 51% of employers have disciplined or terminated workers for violating e-policy.[5]

8-9. Research shows 60% of employees engage in adult-oriented e-mail at work, and 55% send or receive politically incorrect or otherwise offensive e-mail at work.[6] Doing so places employees at risk of disciplinary action or termination and sets up their employers for legal claims.

10. True. In fact, nearly 10% of employers have been ordered by courts to produce employee e-mail in the course of workplace lawsuits. Another 10% have defended claims of sexual or racial harassment or discrimination based on employee e-mail use.[7]

11. True. Reduce the likelihood of customer complaints, termination, lawsuits, and other e-disasters by composing well-written, compelling e-mail messages free of offensive, harassing, discriminatory, obscene, menacing, threatening, hostile, or otherwise objectionable language.

P A R T 1

Think Before
You E-Mail

Beware Potential Perils

You may consider the message itself to be the most important part of your e-mail, but there are additional questions to think about before writing. Is e-mail the best way to convey your information? Would a telephone conversation or one-on-one meeting be safer and/or more effective? Is there any chance your e-mail message will come back to haunt you or your employer? Could you or your organization be damaged if your e-mail message were read by an unauthorized reader?

Before writing—and sending—an e-mail message, consider the following:

➤ E-mail is never secure

➤ Big Brother may be reading over your electronic shoulder

➤ Smoking gun e-mail triggers workplace lawsuits

➤ Productivity is lost when cyber-slackers log on

➤ E-mail misuse and abuse may get you fired

➤ E-mail can be e-mbarrassing

➤ E-mail abuse impacts revenues and also reputations

➤ Security breaches cost dollars and jobs

➤ Your employer may sue you

E-Mail Is Never Secure

If you are using e-mail to send personal or confidential messages, beware. E-mail may be the quickest form of written communication, but it is far from the most secure. You may intend to send a confidential e-mail message to one person, but it is easy to hit the wrong key and accidentally send your message to an unintended reader or multiple addresses stored in your electronic address book. If your recipient forwards your message to others, the e-mail you intended as a "for-your-eyes-only" document could be read by dozens, hundreds, perhaps thousands, of strangers.

Real-Life E-Disaster

A young woman in England sent her boyfriend an e-love note complimenting him on an evening of passion. The woman's message was so flattering, her boyfriend decided to forward it to a half-dozen male friends employed by London-based law firms and banks with international offices. Those men in turn forwarded the love-struck woman's message to their friends and colleagues around the world. That very personal e-mail ended up traveling to 10 million computer screens in London, Australia, Hong Kong, and the United States. An international media sensation followed, with The New York Times, Today *show, and media outlets around the globe reporting the story, and the relentless London tabloids driving the mortified writer into hiding.[8]*

Big Brother May Be Reading Over Your Electronic Shoulder

According to a survey conducted by the American Management Association, *US News & World Report,* and The ePolicy Institute, 47% of employers monitor employee e-mail, and 56% are concerned enough about employees' electronic behavior to restrict employees' personal use of the organization's e-mail system.[9] The federal Electronic Communications Privacy Act (ECPA) gives employers the right to monitor all the e-mail traffic on the company's system. Employers who want to protect their organizations' futures and assets are advised to exercise that right. Employees who want to protect their professional reputations and careers are cautioned to use the company's e-mail system as intended—for business purposes only.

Real-Life E-Disaster

Firefighters in Columbus, Ohio, triggered an internal investigation, media sensation, and public uproar when a routine scan of on-the-job Internet surfing revealed that fire division headquarters' staff were visiting as many as 8,000 pornographic sites a day.[10]

Smoking Gun E-Mail Triggers Workplace Lawsuits

When employees write and send inappropriate or offensive e-mail messages, employers often land in court. Nearly 10% of large U.S. employers have had employee e-mail records subpoenaed, and another 10% have battled sexual and racial harassment and discrimination claims stemming from employees' e-mail and Internet use.[11] Many people treat e-mail too casually, writing comments they would never utter aloud. Play it safe. Do not write anything to or about another that you would not feel comfortable saying face-to-face.

Real-Life E-Disaster

In litigation over diet pills manufactured by American Home Products Corporation, some of the most embarrassing evidence against the company came from internal e-mail. In one particularly damaging message, an American Home Products employee expressed dismay at the thought of spending the balance of her career paying off "fat people who are a little afraid of some silly lung problem." The employee's insensitive comment referred to a rare, but often fatal, condition some diet-pill users developed. Such an inappropriate e-mail likely contributed to the company's decision to settle the case in a deal valued at up to $3.75 billion, the largest settlement ever involving a drug company.[12]

Productivity Is Lost When Cyber-Slackers Log On

Are you guilty of using the organization's e-mail system to send personal messages to family, friends and others? If so, you may be in violation of your employer's e-mail policy. Although 39% of employers allow employees full and unrestricted use of office e-mail, 24% ban all personal use of the office e-mail system. And 4% restrict personal e-mail to communications with immediate family. It is no surprise, then, that 46% of employers engage in e-mail and Internet monitoring as a way to gauge employee productivity.[13]

Real-Life E-Disaster

Together, e-mail and Internet abuse take a costly toll on workplace productivity. Nationally, business is estimated to have lost $500 million in workplace productivity in 1999, when Congress released the Starr Report and President Clinton's video deposition over the Internet. Some 13.5 million workers slacked off and logged on to see what the president, Monica Lewinsky, and independent counsel Kenneth Starr had to say about the relationship between the commander-in-chief and the intern.[14]

E-mail Misuse and Abuse May Get You Fired

Inappropriate on-the-job e-mail use can cost employees their professional reputations and jobs. Fully 46% of employers have disciplined and/or terminated employees for sending sexually suggestive or explicit material via office e-mail. Another 28% have disciplined or terminated employees for sending menacing, harassing, discriminatory, or otherwise objectionable e-mail.[15]

Real-Life E-Disaster

The New York Times Company fired 10% of its workforce, nearly two dozen employees, and reprimanded another 20 workers for violating e-mail policy at the company's Norfolk, Virginia, Shared Services Center. Most of the employees, terminated for sending and/or receiving e-mails that included sexual images and offensive jokes, were otherwise in good standing. In fact, one of the offenders recently had received a promotion, and another had been named "employee of the quarter" before termination.[16] A prime example of bad e-mail decimating a seemingly good workforce.

E-Mail Can Be E-mbarrassing

One individual with poor judgment or a lack of regard for the company's computer resources can trigger a high-profile disaster that can embarrass employees, employers, and shareholders alike.

Real-Life E-Disaster

When a Federal Communications Commission (FCC) employee inadvertently sent a dirty joke titled "Nuns in Heaven" to 6,000 journalists and government officials, the joke was on the FCC. Rather than e-mailing the joke to his intended reader (a friend), the employee (responsible for mailing the FCC's "Daily Digest" to this same group of 6,000) inadvertently sent the off-color joke to every reporter and decision-maker on the agency's group list. One employee's lapse in judgment and electronic mistake resulted in negative publicity and national embarrassment for the FCC.[17]

E-Mail Abuse Impacts Revenues and Also Reputations

E-mail misuse and abuse carries a hefty price tag. Including legal fees and settlement costs, lost productivity and wasted computer resources, stolen data and sabotaged computer equipment, employers put their organizations' financial assets and futures at risk whenever employees access the organization's e-mail system. And it is not just staff who trigger e-disasters. Without comprehensive training such as that provided in these pages, any e-mail user—from the CEO to the summer intern—puts the company at risk of a costly e-mail disaster.

Real-Life E-Disaster

When the CEO of Cerner Corporation sent an angry e-mail berating managers for lackluster performance, he never anticipated the message would be read by anyone other than the 400 managers to whom it was addressed. Unfortunately, one recipient's decision to post the CEO's message on Yahoo!® increased readership to include the company's 3,100 employees, along with financial analysts, investors, and others with an interest in the publicly traded company. The result of the CEO's electronic tirade: Cerner's stock valuation dropped 22% in just three days.[18]

Security Breaches Cost Dollars and Jobs

Research shows one in 10 employees has received confidential company information via e-mail. Fully 79% of employees admit to sharing confidential information with other companies via e-mail.[19]

Real-Life E-Disaster

Shortly before the Persian Gulf War, a London thief grabbed a laptop computer from a parked car belonging to a British military officer. Eventually the computer was recovered. But, with classified material supposedly on the machine's hard drive, the officer was court-martialed and demoted.[20]

Your Employer May Sue You

Workers beware. Employers are no longer the only ones who are getting into legal hot water, thanks to inappropriate e-mail. Now employers are taking legal action against employees who defame and/or harass the company electronically.

Deciding When to Use E-Mail[21]

E-mail is quick and convenient, but it is not always the best means of communication. Before you write your first electronic word, think about your message and intended reader. Consider any outside factors—language barriers, time zone differences, and hidden readers—that could affect how your electronic message is received. Then determine whether the message would be communicated best by e-mail or telephone or in a face-to-face meeting.

Avoid E-Mail When:

➤ Your message is extremely important or confidential and you cannot risk a breach of privacy. If you are not willing to have your words read by an unintended audience, do not use e-mail. It is simply not secure.

➤ You need to deliver unpleasant news and do not want to appear cold or indifferent. As a rule, deliver bad news in person or over the telephone. This gives you the opportunity to warm up your message with appropriate facial expressions, body language, and vocal inflection. For example, e-mail would be the most effective way to notify the accounting department of a mandatory staff meeting. But the meeting itself—not a cold, impersonal e-mail message—would be the appropriate place to break the news that the department is being downsized.

➤ There is a chance your written message would be misunderstood or misconstrued.

➤ You need an immediate response. E-mail may be the best way to deliver news fast, but it is not necessarily the best route to a quick reply. For an immediate response to a pressing issue or question, use the telephone or meet face-to-face.

➤ You want to conduct negotiations or hold a give-and-take conversation. Whether you want to negotiate a price reduction with a supplier or persuade your supervisor to give you a pay raise, conversations that call for back-and-forth discussion would best take place over the phone or in person.

➤ You need to conduct a lengthy interview with a long list of questions that call for detailed answers.

➤ You seek a timely response from someone who may not check e-mail regularly or who has a tendency to procrastinate.

➤ You want to involve several people in your discussion. Such a scenario calls for a teleconference, discussion-group software, or a bulletin-board system rather than e-mail.

➤ You run the risk of intimidating or turning off the reader with a written message.

Use E-Mail When:

➤ You want to deliver a message quickly, and the speed with which you receive your reply does not matter. Remember, your reader is under no obligation to open, read, or act upon your message in a timely fashion.

➤ You want to communicate directly with the decision-maker, rather than fight your way past a gatekeeper. As long as you have the decision-maker's correct e-mail address, there is a good chance your message will be read by your intended reader.

Bear in mind, however, that not all managers read and respond to their own e-mail. A survey conducted by the International Association of Administrative Professionals and The ePolicy Institute reveals that 26% of administrative professionals screen incoming e-mail for executives. Another 29% of assistants are authorized to delete e-mail addressed to the manager.[22]

➤ You want to avoid the cost of long-distance phone calls and faxes, local or overnight delivery services, or snail mail.

➤ You need to communicate with a colleague or a customer in a different time zone or country, and you do not want to make a phone call in the middle of the night. Thanks to e-mail, both the sender and the receiver can conduct business during normal working hours.

➤ You want to deliver the same message to multiple readers. Whether it is a memo intended for six readers or an e-mail newsletter going to 6,000 subscribers, e-mail makes it easy to deliver news quickly, easily, and inexpensively.

➤ You need to maintain a written record of your electronic conversation. Before saving a message, however, review the company's document retention and deletion policy and/or ask your supervisor for authorization to store the e-mail.

➤ You are on a tight deadline. If an assignment is due on the president's desk at 8:00 Monday morning, you can work all weekend, send the document Sunday night, and sleep soundly, knowing your material is sitting in the recipient's mailbox, awaiting review.

Be careful, however, not to wait until the last minute. Delays and delivery problems sometimes occur. Although the majority of messages are delivered without problems, the possibility always exists that your recipient's mail server will be down, keeping your message from getting through.

➤ You want to communicate quickly and cost-effectively with co-workers. Why waste paper and time writing and distributing hard copies of memos when you can send internal e-mail messages with the click of your mouse? Just remember that the organization's netiquette and cyberlanguage guidelines apply to internal e-mail as well as external correspondence.

➤ You need to stay in touch with your office and customers while you are on the road. E-mail can be accessed from anywhere, as long as you can log onto the Internet (see the Directory of E-Mail Hardware in the Appendix). E-mail communication beats phone tag any time, particularly for weary travelers caught between flight schedules, time zones, and competing priorities.

Addressing Your E-Mail Message

Distributing e-mail is different from sending traditional (snail) mail. With snail mail, you simply address an envelope to each recipient, then drop your letters in a mailbox. With e-mail, even the act of addressing a message takes forethought because you have the option of sending the same message to one person or an entire group of readers.

Sending E-Mail to Individual Recipients

There are two ways to address messages to individual recipients:

➤ Write the recipient's e-mail address on the address line every time you send a message. This is an easy method if you rarely e-mail the recipient, but inefficient when you repeatedly communicate with someone, unless your e-mail software is equipped with a memory feature that suggests frequently used addresses based on the first character(s) you type.

➤ Use an electronic address book. Almost all e-mail packages allow users to create an address book with the names and e-mail addresses of people frequently contacted. Simply select a name from your electronic address book and your software does the addressing work for you.

Reaching Multiple Readers

Most e-mail software allows you to send copies and blind carbon copies of your messages. Generally, it is as easy as selecting *To, Cc,* or *Bcc* when addressing your e-mail.

E-Mail Address Element	Definition
To	Use this option for the primary recipient(s) of your message.
Cc	*Cc* is shorthand for carbon copy. Enter the address of anyone you would like to receive a copy of your e-mail on the *Cc* line. Avoid controversy and hurt feelings by alphabetizing the list of *Cc* recipients.
Bcc	*Bcc* means blind carbon copy. If you want to send a copy of your e-mail without the original recipient's knowledge, put the address on the *Bcc* line. Or if you want to send a completely "blind" message, enter all recipients' e-mail addresses on the *Bcc* line.

User Tips for *Cc* and *Bcc* Options

➤ Using the *Bcc* option can control the flow of replies to your e-mail message. When you enter all your recipients' names on the *Bcc* line (and leave *To* and *Cc* blank), all replies come to you alone, rather than to recipients of your original message.

Let's say, for example, you e-mail 300 employees to announce that the company no longer permits casual dress on Fridays. If one disgruntled employee were to click "reply all" and send an angry message expressing his disregard for management and disrespect for company policies, you would be the sole recipient of the employee's hostile tirade. Computer resources and productivity would be saved, and organization-wide dissent would be averted.

➤   Just because it is possible to send carbon copies and blind carbon copies does not make it appropriate in all circumstances. Send copies only to those who need to read your document. E-mail users are inundated with legitimate correspondence and junk mail. Sending a copy to someone who does not need to read your message wastes everyone's time.

➤   Carbon-copy recipients are not required to reply to messages. Do not get upset when a response is not forthcoming.

➤   Blind carbon copies pose an additional challenge. If you inadvertently click *Cc* when you meant *Bcc,* you risk exposing yourself to complaints and possible lawsuits. Not only will readers be annoyed when they have to scroll through your *Cc* list (which could number in the hundreds or more), but the wholesale distribution of e-mail addresses could trigger a lawsuit on the grounds that confidentiality was breached or privacy violated.

Real-Life E-Disaster

As a service to patients, a pharmaceutical company that manufactures a popular antidepressant drug publishes an electronic newsletter devoted to the care and treatment of depression and nervous conditions. An e-mail subscription feature ensures the newsletter is received only by those who sign up for it. A Bcc mailing list had always guaranteed patient anonymity—until the day a pharmaceutical company employee accidentally hit the Cc button, making thousands of confidential e-mail addresses public. The potential for liability was huge, as patients being treated for depression faced a breach of privacy and the fear that unscrupulous marketers would capitalize on the no-longer-confidential address list.

Using Group Lists

Many e-mail software packages allow you to create and maintain group lists. If, for example, you frequently send e-mail to the members of your project team, you could add their names and e-mail addresses to a group list labeled "project team." When you want to e-mail the entire team, simply select the group name, and the addressing is completed for you.

As a first step, however, check your organization's e-mail policy for prohibitions against the use of group lists or mass e-mailings to company employees.

Listserv® Guidelines

Similarly, refer to your written e-mail policy before subscribing to a Listserv. Listservs are subscription-only e-mail lists that allow large numbers of participants to share information and discuss issues. If you belong to a professional association, for instance, you may sign up for that association's Listserv.

Although Listservs are a quick and convenient way to share information and hold electronic discussions, they can create problems for the recipient and the recipient's employer. A Listserv may have many, many subscribers. Every message and reply that is sent via the Listserv goes to every member. As a result, an employee who belongs to just one Listserv could receive many messages on any given day. Should that employee join several Listservs, the volume could increase to hundreds of e-mail messages a day. Multiply the time and resources spent by one Listserv subscriber by the total number of employees in your organization, and you could be facing a productivity nightmare.

Employers are advised to reduce the burden on their e-mail servers and control employees' online time by establishing guidelines to prohibit Listserv participation. Some organizations ban Listservs altogether or restrict subscriptions to authorized, business-related Listservs.[23]

Replying to E-Mail Messages

Often it is more convenient and appropriate to reply to a received message than to write and address a brand-new one. Replying to a message is as easy as clicking on *Reply*. The *To* and *From* lines are reversed so the addressing work is completed, and the original message may be displayed, if you have set up this option in your e-mail program.

It is usually advisable to leave the original subject line intact, even if your reply changes the subject. Doing so provides continuity for the original writer and any intended and hidden readers you pick up along the way.

If your software allows you to forward your reply to other readers, click *Forward*, write the new addresses on the appropriate *To, Cc,* or *Bcc* lines, and then click *Send*.

Always include a salutation and signature to ensure that your comments are identifiable, no matter how many times the message is appended and forwarded. These elements are covered in more detail in Part 2.

Formatting Your Reply

Should you write your reply above, below, or within the original message? In most cases, you will write your reply above the sender's message, leaving the original copy intact for reference. The placement of your message at the top enables the reader to locate it quickly and easily. Your salutation *(Dear Ali)* and signature *(Cordially, Truman)* clearly mark where your reply message begins and ends. You can also give your comments a distinctive look by changing the color of your text or placing asterisks, symbolizing *italics,* on each side of your remarks.

When you need to respond to a list of questions, open your reply with a brief notice that your answers are contained within the body of the original message. This will save the reader the trouble of scrolling to the end of the screen in search of your answers. Then simply type your answers immediately after each respective question. Introduce your answers with your initials, the word *answer,* an uppercase *A,* or another clue directing the reader to your comments.

Requesting a Receipt

Suppose you have written a crucial message that absolutely must be delivered. Short of receiving a response, how can you be certain your message has been received and read?

The quickest, easiest route to peace of mind is to select the receipt notification option on your screen. When the reader opens your message, you will be notified automatically. Many e-mail packages offer this feature. But software incompatibility can inhibit notification.

Think about your reader before choosing the receipt notification option. Readers may resent the implication that you do not trust them to open their e-mail. In a pressing situation, the better option might be to phone your recipient with a quick heads-up that the message is on its way and you would appreciate a timely response.

Real-Life E-Disaster

Lockheed Martin's e-mail system crashed for six hours after an employee sent 60,000 co-workers a personal e-mail about a national day of prayer, complete with a request for an electronic receipt. The defense contractor, which posts 40 million e-mails monthly, lost hundreds of thousands of dollars thanks to this one employee's action and the resulting system crash.

Before Lockheed Martin's e-crisis passed, a Microsoft rescue squad was flown in to repair the damage to the company's e-mail system and ensure such an e-time bomb would never detonate again. The employee responsible for Lockheed Martin's e-disaster was fired for committing an act of sabotage.[24]

Sending a Priority Message

Many e-mail packages allow you to assign high, normal, or low priority messages. Not a means of speeding electronic delivery, the priority designation simply alerts readers to the presence of an important message. Use the priority feature judiciously. If every message you send carries the high-priority designation, readers will begin to disregard the label and question the importance of all your correspondence.

E-Mailing to International Audiences

One of the beauties of e-mail is that it enables you to communicate quickly and easily with colleagues and customers around the globe. If you will be communicating electronically with readers in other countries, apply the following tips for effective international e-mail:

➤ International electronic communication poses unique language, cultural, and time challenges. Think about your international reader's communication needs before writing and sending a message abroad.

➤ English may be the international language of commerce, but that does not mean every reader, intended and hidden, will have a trouble-free experience with messages written in English. Determine who your reader is and what your reader's needs are before you start writing. If necessary, have your message translated into the language(s) best understood by your intended reader(s).

➤ International e-mail calls for more detailed and specific information than does local e-mail. For example, a message that reads, "Our video conference will begin at 6 P.M. on 6/5/03," could have unfortunate results. Americans would read the date as June 5, 2003. Europeans would interpret it as May 6, 2003. And the Japanese, using a year/month/day order, would face more confusion.

Because Europeans use a 24-hour military clock, be sure to write international e-mail in that format, thus: "The video conference will begin at 18:00 on 5 June 2003."

Similarly, when sending domestic e-mail to business associates in other parts of the United States, be sure to indicate time zone, such as Eastern Standard Time (EST) or Central Daylight Time (CDT).

Measurements can prove equally challenging when sending e-mail internationally. To eliminate confusion, give the metric measurement, followed by its American equivalent in parentheses. For example, "Paul ran a 10-kilometer (6.2-mile) road race on Saturday."

➤ Do not assume all speakers of a given language are culturally similar. English-speaking Americans differ culturally from the English-speaking populations of Australia, Ireland, and Canada. For that matter, some English-speaking Americans differ culturally from other English-speaking Americans who live in a different part of the country or have different ethnic backgrounds. So too do Spanish-speaking Mexicans differ culturally from Spaniards, and French-speaking Canadians differ culturally from the French.

➤ Even if you are sending an e-mail to an employee at one of your organization's own international locations, avoid using technical language, jargon, acronyms, abbreviations, or humor. Given language and cultural differences, there is too much opportunity for misunderstanding and confusion.

➤ Be specific and avoid vague language. American references and terms, such as *Midwest* and *West Coast* or *junior high* and *middle school,* are too vague for many international readers. Also be mindful of terms that change in meaning depending upon the country in which they are used. In the United States, for example, a *boot* is a type of shoe. In the United Kingdom, a *boot* is the trunk of a car. Word choice plays a significant role in the clarity of communication and the overall effectiveness of e-mail.

Composing Your
E-Mail Message

Collecting Your Thoughts with the Five Ws

During a business day, e-mail users may receive many, many messages. The competition to capture the attention and interest of the electronic reader is fierce. Just as newspaper writers vie with many other writers to capture their readers' attention, you too are competing with many other e-mail correspondents to ensure that your message is opened, read, and acted upon. So it makes sense to borrow some techniques of journalistic writing to apply to composing e-mail messages.

To collect your thoughts before you write, answer the journalist's five Ws: *who, what, when, where,* and *why.*

➤ *Who* is your reader? How much does the reader know about your subject? What prejudices does the reader have that could influence acceptance of your document? How does the reader feel about you? How experienced is your reader with e-mail? What will it take to convince the reader to act?

➤ *What* is the primary purpose of your e-mail? Are you trying to persuade readers to act, inform them of a problem or event, elicit a response to a question? Do you have more than one purpose?

➤ *When* does the action take place? Does the reader need to be concerned about a deadline? Do you need to provide a meeting time?

➤ *Where* does the action take place? Do you need to provide an address or directions? Before writing, gather every fact the reader needs to make a decision.

➤ *Why* should the reader care about your e-mail message? How interested in your topic is the reader? Will the reader benefit by acting on your document? Will there be negative fallout if the reader does not act? Think about your message from the reader's point of view, and communicate benefits early in the document.

Answering the five Ws before you begin writing helps you determine the exact elements you need to communicate so you do not forget something important. Armed with these main points, you can move on to draft an attention-getting subject line and a well-conceived e-mail message.

Writing Subject Lines with Real Oomph

The subject line is the first clue an e-mail recipient has about the importance of your message. Typically, a reader's e-mail inbox will display only the brief subject line of each message received. Writers often compose subject lines that are too vague, boring, or cute to be effective. With a little effort, however, you can learn to write subject lines with real oomph that make your e-mail messages stand out.

Tips for Writing Powerful Subject Lines

➤ **State your message clearly, concisely, and descriptively.**
A subject line that reads "Quarterly Results" does not have the impact of "Third Quarter Sales Up 15%." A descriptive subject line draws the reader to the message by providing an accurate sense of what you have to say before the message itself is opened and read.

➤ **Consider your primary audience when writing the subject line, but do not overdo it.** Resist the urge to use jargon, acronyms, or technical terms, even if you are certain the reader will understand. You want to entice readers, not scare them away before they start reading.

➤ **Remember the hidden reader.** When messages are forwarded from one reader to the next, the original subject line often is left intact. This gives you the opportunity to attract a broader audience of unintended readers to your message.

➤ **Do not use the subject line to oversell your message or trick the reader.** A reader may fall for a misleading subject line once, but the next message you send might be ignored or deleted before it is read.

➤ **Steer clear of subject lines commonly used for spam, or junk e-mail.** A legitimate e-mail, if accompanied by one of the subject lines below, is likely to be trashed by a busy reader who scans subject lines to determine which messages to open and which to delete. Avoid using these in your subject lines: "Information," "Just for You," "Thank You," "Have You Seen This?," "Great Opportunity," "Free Gift," "Read This Now." Also, avoid any mention of sex, hot photos, adults only, weight loss, or moneymaking opportunities.

Serving Multiple Audiences with a Single Subject Line

To send a single message to many people with varying needs and interests, write a subject line that appeals to everyone.

Let's say your supervisor asks you to send an e-mail memo inviting members of the accounting and information systems departments to a demonstration of a new accounting software package. If you write a subject line that reads "Accounting Software Demo," the information systems department might assume the demo does not pertain to them and delete the memo without reading it. If, on the other hand, your subject line reads "Technical Perspectives of Accounting Software," the accountants might be scared away.

The solution: Write a subject line that appeals to both audiences. "Demo of Accounting & Tech Aspects of New Software" might result in a solid turnout from both departments.

Draft a Subject Line

For the examples that follow, practice writing single subject lines to reach multiple audiences. Limit your subject lines to a maximum of six words.

1. An internal e-mail is to instruct employees to attend a mandatory meeting in which the organization's new e-mail policy will be introduced. Your goal is to generate 100% employee attendance at the meeting.

   _____

2. An external e-mail is to introduce customers and prospects to the organization's new line of state-of-the-art products. Your goal is to motivate readers to open the attached product brochure.

   _____

Compare your answers with the authors' suggested responses in the Appendix.

Incorporating a Salutation and Signature

Because you never can be certain where your e-mail message will land—possibly on the screens of co-workers, supervisors, customers, vendors, and others—it is advisable to include a salutation and signature in every important message. This allows hidden readers to follow your message's trail, mindful of the original sender and recipient. It is also good to include a salutation and signature when you are forwarding messages. Identify your intended recipient, explain in a line or two why you are passing along the message, and sign your name. Doing so will establish your role in the electronic document's history, regardless of how many times it is forwarded.

Another benefit: Your signature signals the end of the message, sparing readers the annoyance of scrolling to the end of the screen to see if there is more copy.

Creating a Signature File

Many e-mail packages allow you to add a customized signature to all your messages, eliminating the need to re-enter copy each time. In fact, your software may allow you to create a number of signature files, reflecting the different professional hats you wear: employee, industry association board member, and so on.

When creating a signature file, do your readers the courtesy of including comprehensive contact information, including your company name and address, phone and fax numbers, e-mail address/hyperlink, and Web address/hyperlink. That way, if the reader wants to contact you in any way other than return e-mail, all the necessary contact information is at hand. For example:

```
Bridget F. Schodorf
Vice President
The ePolicy Institute
2300 Walhaven Court, Suite 200A
Columbus, Ohio, USA 43220
614/451-3200 (phone)
614/451-8726 (fax)
experts@epolicyinstitute.com
www.epolicyinstitute.com
```

In informal correspondence, or in an ongoing series of back-and-forth messages between the same two people, a less formal sign-off is appropriate. Your name (first name or first and last, depending upon how well you know the reader), preceded by *Best, Cordially, Regards,* or a similar sign-off, will help warm up your correspondence, while still providing a stop sign for your reader.

Grabbing the Reader's Attention: The Lead

To maximize the impact of any written document, electronic or traditional, you must start strong. The lead—beginning with the first word of the first sentence and ending at the conclusion of the first paragraph—is the writer's best, and sometimes only, opportunity to grab the reader's attention.

A well-conceived lead draws readers in, motivating them to read the document through to its conclusion. If the lead is well written, your reader will grasp your meaning right away and decide immediately whether to continue reading, save your document for later review, or delete it.

Understanding the Lead's Role

> ➤ The lead structures your message. It leaves the reader no doubt about why you have written it or whether to continue reading.

> ➤ The lead delivers the document's most important, compelling information right up front, often in the form of a conclusion.

> ➤ The lead summarizes what is to come later in the document.

> ➤ The lead captures—and holds—the reader's attention.

Sample Leads, Weak and Strong

Here are two examples of weak leads, along with suggested revisions.

Weak Lead #1

```
Of LLF & Associates' 2,500 employees, approximately 2,000 are
using the company's e-mail system on a regular basis. The problem
is that many of the 2,000 persons enjoying the company's e-mail
are using it for personal correspondence. Management is aware this
is going on and wants it stopped. As of January 1, the e-mail
system of LLF & Associates is reserved for business use. Any em-
ployee caught using it for personal reasons will be put on proba-
tion. Three violations of the new e-mail policy will result in
termination.
```

Analysis: This weak lead contains too much unnecessary and secondary information, all of which appears at the beginning of the paragraph. The reader does not learn until the final three sentences that the company is instituting a tough new e-mail policy.

Revised Lead #1

Effective January 1, personal use of LLF & Associates' corporate e-mail is prohibited. Employees who violate this e-mail policy by making personal use of the system will be put on immediate probation. Three violations will result in termination.

Analysis: This strong lead tells readers what they need to know. A busy reader can grasp the message's meaning immediately.

Weak Lead #2

This is a response I have written to Gloria, who recently shared her thoughts about her concerns for our association and our board. I think she has raised important issues that we must address. I send it to you because Tim and I believe we absolutely need a strategic planning session no later than December.

Analysis: The writer wastes valuable time describing the e-mail message to the reader (This is a response I have written...; I send it to you because...), rather than simply delivering the message. A well-written message should be strong enough to stand alone without any introduction.

Revised Lead #2

Tim, Gloria, and I agree our association faces enormous challenges. Let's hold a strategic planning session by December to review board members' concerns and begin planning for the future.

Analysis: At 29 words, this strong lead is nearly half the length of the 55-word original. Succinct and to the point, this lead conveys the writer's thoughts clearly and quickly.

STRENGTHEN THE LEAD

As you read this weak lead, think about how you might edit it to make the paragraph more powerful and meaningful to a busy reader.

Jane Tomm, a graduate of State University, with a master's in journalism and a bachelor's in English, is an integral member of the Health Department's public relations team, serving initially as a public information officer then as manager of special projects. An employee of the state for 12 years, Jane also has published two books of children's fiction and is a volunteer tutor with the city schools, teaching writing skills to high school students. Effective today, Jane has been named communications chief for the State Health Department. All supervisors, managers, and staff will begin reporting to Jane immediately. Please plan to attend tomorrow's 7 A.M. staff meeting to learn more about Jane's promotion and her plans for the department.

Identify the meat of the message. What are the three most important sentences in the paragraph? List them in order of importance, with item 1 being the most important.

1._____

2._____

3._____

Now delete all the unnecessary information and rewrite the paragraph using the three sentences you identified as your lead.

_____

_____

_____

_____

Compare your answers with the authors' suggested responses in the Appendix.

Organizing with the Inverted Pyramid

Like good journalistic writing, good business writing is structured as an inverted, or upside-down, pyramid. The most important information is communicated right up front, in the lead. Following the lead, information is presented in descending order of importance.

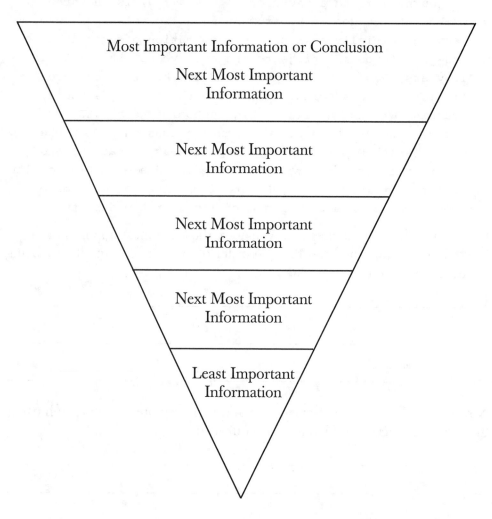

Most Important Information or Conclusion

Next Most Important Information

Next Most Important Information

Next Most Important Information

Next Most Important Information

Least Important Information

Why take an inverted pyramid approach to writing e-mail? Deluged with electronic and traditional correspondence, few business people have time to read every word of every memo, letter, and proposal that crosses their computer screens or lands on their desks.

How does a harried reader decide which e-mail documents to read and respond to, and which to delete from the screen? Typically the reader scans the lead—the first few words and sentences—and then decides whether to continue reading. This is why it is so important to deliver your primary message right up front, at the beginning of your e-mail document. Before writing, think about your goal. Do you want to alert readers to a problem? Notify your staff about a rescheduled meeting? Persuade your supervisor to increase your department's budget?

Formula for E-Mail Success

Whatever your objective in writing your e-mail message, apply the following formula to organize your communication for maximum effectiveness:

1. Restrict each e-mail to one primary message—the one action you want the reader to take.

2. Lead with your primary message.

3. Focus on your first three sentences. By the end of sentence three, readers should have no doubt what your message is about or what action they are expected to take.

4. Repeat, rephrase, and reiterate. Use the balance of your e-mail to drive home the point you made so succinctly and effectively in sentences one through three.

5. Limit e-mail messages to a maximum of one screen page. If you need more room, consider adding an attachment.

Comparing Chronological Writing

Many writers, who may be unfamiliar with the inverted pyramid approach, format their writing chronologically. The problem with most chronological writing, however, is that it takes the reader too long to get to the good stuff. Consider, for example, this chronological message from a college student looking for a post-graduation job:

Letter with Chronological Format

Dear Personnel Manager:

My name is Matt Kennedy. I'm a 22-year-old college senior who will graduate from State University this June with a degree in English.

During my four years at SU, I served first as a writer for, then as the editor of, the university's literary magazine. In addition, as a junior, I was a sports columnist for SU's student newspaper, *The Beacon*.

My university-level editorial work was a natural offshoot of my experience at City High School. During my tenure at CHS, I was actively involved as a member of the school's yearbook and newspaper staffs.

It is no surprise that my academic career has focused so extensively on communications. I did, after all, publish my first book when I was a mere eighth-grader. Co-authored by my mother and published by Scribners, that fictional children's work is now in its second printing.

I would like to put my communications experience to work for XYZ Company. I hope you will consider me for an entry-level position in your public relations department.

Sincerely,

Matt Kennedy

Analysis: This chronological message is written in mystery-writer style. Not until the final paragraph does the personnel manager learn what Matt wants. Matt gambles that the reader will stick with him to the end. Given the weakness of his lead and the potential for boredom inherent in chronological writing, Matt is taking a big risk sending this e-mail message to a busy personnel manager.

Letter with Inverted Pyramid Format

Dear Personnel Manager:

Would a published author with eight years of experience as a writer and editor be a valuable addition to your company's public relations staff? If that communicator were a 22-year-old looking for an entry-level position to get his career off to a terrific start, would you be interested? I'm Matt Kennedy, and as you can tell, I have packed a lot of experience into the first two decades of my life. I'd now like to put that experience to work for XYZ Company.

A senior at State University, set to receive a bachelor's degree in English this June, I am seeking an entry-level position in XYZ Company's public relations department. What assets would I bring to XYZ?

1. **Professionalism:** I published my first fictional children's book in the eighth grade. Co-authored by my mother and published by Scribners, that book is now in its second printing.

2. **Teamwork:** I served on the staffs of SU's literary magazine and student newspaper. In high school, I worked on the yearbook and newspaper staffs. I understand how to work as a part of a team of writers, editors, designers, and photographers.

3. **Leadership:** As the editor of SU's literary magazine, I developed a knack for motivating staff and an understanding of what it takes to complete a project on deadline and within budget.

I hope to have the opportunity to meet with you in the near future.

Sincerely,

Matt Kennedy

Analysis: This e-mail message has real oomph. Matt makes it clear in the first paragraph that he is looking for an entry-level PR position. Thanks to his unique and powerful lead, he distinguishes himself from other's hoping to get a foot in the door at XYZ Company. The short, numbered paragraphs with bold headlines makes his message easy to read, understand, and act upon.

Getting Started in Three Easy Steps

For many people, the hardest part of writing is getting started. The thought of writing the first few words in the all-important lead sentence paralyzes many writers. Do not let a blank screen intimidate you. Apply this three-step trick for getting started.

1 Begin your lead sentence with a well-worn cliché such as "The purpose of this memo is," or "I am writing today because," or "In response to your e-mail of April 1," or "Thank you."

2 Complete your first sentence by attaching your primary message to the cliché you selected to jump-start the writing process. Then continue writing your document, inverted-pyramid style.

3 When you are finished writing, return to the first sentence and replace your opening cliché with a stylish, attention-getting phrase. Make any necessary changes to the rest of the message.

The result: a first sentence that is likely to grab the reader's attention precisely because it does not begin with a tired old phrase the reader has seen on the screen time and time again.

Example:

Step 1: The purpose of this e-mail message is

Step 2: The purpose of this e-mail message is to share my belief that the ad agency must be replaced. Our market share has dropped 29% over the past nine months, and the agency has offered no solutions. Let's discuss at next week's board meeting.

Step 3: The ad agency must be replaced. Our market share has dropped 29% over the past nine months, and the agency has offered no solutions. Let's discuss at next week's board meeting.

Keys to Effective

E-Mail

34

Striving for Simplicity

Composing an electronic memo is no different from writing other business correspondence in many ways: It must be clear, concise, and inoffensive to the reader. Despite the instant nature of e-mail, it is still necessary to keep the reader's attention. Working through this chapter will help you write e-mail that will get your message across—and keep your documents out of the reader's electronic recycle bin!

Maximize the effectiveness of your e-mail by keeping your writing short and simple. In electronic writing, as in all business writing, no prize is given for the longest word or the most complex sentence. Big words and overly long sentences seldom impress readers. And a reader who is confused or irritated is less likely to respond to your message.

Do yourself and your readers a favor by selecting short, familiar words. The same holds true for sentence structure.

The Benefits of Short, Simple Sentences

➤ Short sentences are easier to write, read, and understand. Long sentences, always more difficult to read, are particularly hard to read on-screen.

➤ Long sentences test the writer's ability to use grammar and punctuation correctly. A hurried e-mail reader is more likely to delete a confusing, error-filled message than take time to plow through the writer's mechanical errors and decipher the document's meaning.

➤ Long sentences tend to bury ideas. Remember the inverted pyramid. Put short sentences and paragraphs to work, communicating your primary message clearly, right from the beginning of the document.

➤ Limit most sentences to one major idea.

For more information on writing clearly and concisely, read *Fat-Free Writing* by Carol Andrus, Crisp Publications.

Editing to be Concise

The following long, wordy, heavily punctuated sentence challenges the recipient's ability to read and understand what the writer is saying. Could you blame the reader for deleting this message from the screen?

```
I am writing this e-mail memo to confirm that the highway de-
partment will begin work on the repaving of Main Street the week
of May 1, and we hope to complete the job within 30 days, but
you need to be aware of the fact that weather conditions will
impact our ability to start and finish on time, so if we experi-
ence a particularly rainy or cold spring, we may not be able to
meet the June 1 deadline set forth by city council.
```

Begin your editing process by underlining the main point(s) and circling any unnecessary coordinating conjunctions (and, or, nor, for, but, so, yet), commas, and words. In our version, which follows, we have used bold to indicate unnecessary conjunctions and italics for unnecessary words:

```
I am writing this e-mail memo to confirm that the highway de-
partment will begin work on the repaving of Main Street the week
of May 1, and we hope to complete the job within 30 days, but
you need to be aware of the fact that weather conditions will
impact our ability to start and finish on time, so if we experi-
ence a particularly rainy or cold spring, we may not be able to
meet the June 1 deadline set forth by city council.
```

Now rewrite the sentence, deleting unnecessary conjunctions, words, and phrases. The result? A short, simple sentence.

```
The highway department will begin repaving Main Street the week
of May 1, completing the job by city council's June 1 deadline,
barring weather delays.
```

Another option works equally well. Write two short sentences.

```
The highway department will begin repaving Main Street the week
of May 1. Unless the weather delays us, we will complete the job
within the city council's 30-day deadline.
```

REWRITE FOR READABILITY

The following sentences are too long. Underline the main point(s) of each sentence and place brackets around needless words or phrases. Then rewrite as short, readable sentences. Be sure to lead with the most important information.

1. The Yummy Pet Food Company is looking for 100 consumers to participate in an online survey of pet-food buying habits, and we are willing to pay each participant $100 for his or her time and trouble, but we must begin our survey next Monday, so, if you are interested in participating, please e-mail us today, sending your e-mail to the attention of Miss Kitty Paas, kpaas@yummypfc.com, in the marketing department.

   _____

   _____

2. This e-mail message has been written to alert all my clients of my new e-mail address, ali@epolicyinstitute.com, which becomes effective January 1, and will make me available to respond to client needs more quickly, but if, in the interim, you need to reach me, please do not hesitate to contact me the good old-fashioned way, via voicemail.

   _____

   _____

3. Please do not use the company's e-mail system for personal purposes, such as advertising cars and other items for sale, or notifying co-workers of the birth or wedding of a child, and please remember that this e-mail system is monitored by management, and we will not tolerate the use of off-color language, offensive jokes, or other inappropriate material, and if the personal and inappropriate use of the corporate e-mail does not come to an end, we will be forced to take disciplinary action against the violators, so knock it off.

   _____

   _____

Compare your answers with the authors' suggested responses in the Appendix.

Writing with Power...or Paste?

One of the most effective ways to develop a clean, clear writing style is to eliminate surplus words from your sentences. There are two types of words in a writer's arsenal:

➤ *Power* words convey the meaning of your sentences.

➤ *Paste* words hold your sentences together as tight, grammatical units.

Your goal is to write sentences that contain more power than paste. The following *pasty* sentences create a weak paragraph:

```
This is a response I have written to one customer who recently
shared his thoughts about his concerns for our return policy. I
send it to you because I believe we need to develop and imple-
ment a more customer-oriented approach to service.
```

Let's analyze these sentences, underlining the power words and highlighting the paste words with italic type:

```
This is a response I have written to one customer who recently
shared his thoughts about his concerns for our return policy. I
send it to you because I believe we need to develop and imple-
ment a more customer-oriented approach to service.
```

These two sentences together contain 21 power words and 22 paste words. That is too much paste. The writer's primary message—the need to develop and implement a more customer-oriented approach to service—comes at the end of the paragraph. In keeping with the inverted pyramid format, the writer's main message should lead the paragraph:

```
We need to develop and implement more customer-oriented service.
As one concerned customer recently said of our return policy...
```

RUB OUT THE PASTE

For the following exercise, underline the power words, bracket the paste, and tally each. Rewrite the sentences, eliminating as much paste as possible and making any changes necessary to strengthen each sentence.

1. In the event that the building loses power and the lights go off during working hours, all employees are instructed to remain seated at their desks and await the instructions of the department manager who is assigned to supervise the activity of the department.

   _____ Number of Power Words   _____ Number of Paste Words

   _____

   _____

2. I am sending this e-mail to all members of our association's board of directors to notify each and every member of the board of directors that effective the first of the new year the board will meet every third Monday of each month for the purpose of discussing association business matters.

   _____ Number of Power Words   _____ Number of Paste Words

   _____

   _____

3. Per your e-mail directive of April 1: My understanding is that there is to be no more parking of employee cars in parking spots designated for visitors to the company, nor is there to be any further tolerance of healthy company workers parking their vehicles in spaces that have been designated for disabled persons.

   _____ Number of Power Words   _____ Number of Paste Words

   _____

   _____

Compare your answers with the authors' suggested responses in the Appendix.

Eliminating Mechanical Errors

The *mechanics* of writing are the various principles and rules that make it work—that make it more than a string of independent words. Taught in elementary and high school, many of these particulars about English composition may have been long forgotten by working adults. But a loss of memory for the details makes these points no less important in business writing, including e-mail.

A poorly worded, illogical, or inaccurate e-mail message can drive away customers and destroy sales. All business correspondence—electronic or hard copy—projects an image of you and your organization. In the battle for the reader's on-screen attention, carefully written, thoughtfully worded e-mail free from inappropriate language and mechanical errors is sure to come out on top.

Most reference books on writing address at least the four most commonly used punctuation marks: comma, colon, semicolon, and apostrophe. But e-mail writing commonly includes the use of two other punctuation marks. The following paragraphs explain the appropriate use of the exclamation point and the dash.

➤ **Beware the exclamation point!!!**

Many e-mail writers mistakenly believe they can inject life into their electronic writing by slapping an exclamation point onto the end of every important sentence. Do not fall into this trap!!! Grab reader attention with a compelling subject line. Put power in your writing with descriptive language and well-crafted sentences. Use exclamation points sparingly, if at all.

➤ **Add some dash to your writing.**

Used in place of commas or parentheses, the dash is a handy, versatile punctuation mark used to set off parenthetical material, to indicate breaks in thought, or to separate a phrase needing emphasis.

Note, however, that the standard em-dash (–), so named because it is the width of a capital M, does not translate well electronically. In its place, use two unspaced hyphens (--) with no space before or after.

Example: The intern forgot--if he ever knew--the correct way to address an e-mail message to the Dublin, Ireland, office.

Techniques specifically for improving business correspondence can be found in *Better Business Writing* by Susan L. Brock, Crisp Publications.

Spelling Counts!

Think no one pays attention to electronic spelling? Think again. Even the busiest reader will zero right in on a misspelling. Do not give readers any excuse to discount your document. Spelling errors and typos undermine your credibility and your e-mail's impact. Proofreading on screen is an indispensable part of the electronic writing process.

Five Electronic Spelling Tips

1. **Use your spell-checker program if your e-mail package is equipped with one.** Remember, however, that the electronic spell checker cannot correct usage. For example, it cannot distinguish between to, two, and too; affect and effect; or its and it's. Proofread manually first, using the electronic system for your final check.

2. **Purchase and use a good, up-to-date dictionary.** Besides giving correct spellings, the dictionary is a good reference tool for proper usage and a valuable source of synonyms.

3. **Do not stop writing to look up or spell check every word that looks funny to you.** Wait until your document is completely written, then go back to the beginning and proofread thoroughly.

4. **Take your time with important documents.** Once you push *Send,* your e-mail message is on its way and probably cannot be retrieved. Never put in writing—electronic or traditional—anything that could come back to haunt you. If your document is particularly important or sensitive, you owe it to yourself to slow down and conduct a careful review of spelling, content, and mechanics. If time allows, print and proofread a hard copy before sending your document into cyberspace. When in doubt about the appropriateness of your message, impose a 48-hour cooling-off period before sending it. If time is short, ask a trusted colleague to proofread your message before you send it.

5. **Invest in a writing manual that covers the most commonly misspelled words and typical grammatical goofs.** Writers often confuse word pairs that either sound alike or have similar meanings. The rule to follow is simple: If you have any doubt about the way you are using a word, look it up in the dictionary.

Using the Active Voice

As a rule, business documents should be written in the active, not the passive, voice. Writing in the active voice will ensure that your electronic sentences are shorter, crisper, and easier to read.

Unsure what constitutes the active voice?

Tip 1: In an active construction, the actor, or subject, always appears before the action, or verb. The actor following the action is a telltale sign of a passive sentence.

Tip 2: Watch for the preposition *by*. Its presence almost always signals a passive sentence.

Consider the following passive sentence:

```
It is possible for an audit to be conducted and completed by the
accountants in 30 days.
```

To analyze this sentence, simply ask yourself, "Who is doing what to whom?"

The accountants are the actors [who].
Conduct and complete make up the action [what].
An audit is the object [whom].

Then rewrite the sentence, focusing on these three Ws: *who, what,* and *whom.* The following rewritten, active sentence eliminates all unnecessary words and focuses on actor, action, and object (*who, what,* and *whom*):

```
The accountants can complete an audit in 30 days.
```

Notice that the nine-word active sentence is much shorter than the lumbering 17-word passive sentence. Active constructions are always shorter than the passive. If you write in the active voice, your documents immediately become tighter and more energetic.

ACTIVATE THE SENTENCE

Rewrite these passive sentences, using the active voice and eliminating all unnecessary words. Your goal: Breathe life into these weak constructions.

1. By now the memo should have been received by all intended recipients, and by the end of the week management should be receiving everyone's response via e-mail.

   _____

   _____

   _____

2. Employees who demonstrate adherence to company protocol and procedures shall be rewarded by management when it comes time for performance reviews.

   _____

   _____

   _____

3. Because the pilfering of office supplies by employees is a growing problem at headquarters, the director of human resources is looking for ways to screen job applicants' honesty.

   _____

   _____

   _____

Compare your answers with the authors' suggested responses in the Appendix.

Avoiding Sexist Language

The greater presence of women in business has changed many traditional practices, including the use of language. Historically, English grammar called for masculine pronouns (*he, him, his, himself*) to refer to both men and women. That practice is no longer acceptable. Now writers, including e-mail writers, must look for alternatives to avoid language that could offend clients, colleagues, or hidden readers.

Short of adopting the cumbersome *he/she* or *he* or *she* construction, what's a gender-sensitive e-mail writer to do?

Keeping Your E-Mail Gender-Neutral

➤ **Eliminate the offending pronoun.**

Do not write: The executive should read his e-mail from clients and vendors daily.

Write: The executive should read e-mail sent from clients and vendors daily.

➤ **Repeat the noun and rewrite.**

Do not write: The intern could not understand why the human resources director was so upset when she used the company e-mail system for personal use.

Write: The intern could not understand why the human resources director was so upset when the intern used the company e-mail system for personal use.

➤ **Recast sentences into the plural.**

Do not write: An e-mail writer should use correct grammar and punctuation in his writing.

Write: E-mail writers should use correct grammar and punctuation in their writing.

➤ **Use the generic pronoun, *one*.**

Do not write: A novice computer user is likely to find the local computer retailer and a reputable bookseller his best sources of basic technical information.

Write: A novice computer user is likely to find the local computer retailer and a reputable bookseller one's best sources of basic technical information.

➤ **Rewrite using *who*.**

Do not write: The assumption of many e-mail users is that if a writer corrects his grammar and proofreads his document, he is wasting time.

Write: The assumption of many e-mail users is that a writer who corrects a document's grammar and proofreads it is wasting time.

➤ **Use an article *(a, an, the, this, that, these, those)*.**

Do not write: The contractor received a healthy bonus for his quick, professional work.

Write: The contractor received a healthy bonus for the quick, professional work.

➤ **Use the second person form when appropriate (if you know your audience).**

Do not write: The e-mail writer must take the greatest care when he is using copyrighted reference material.

Write: As an e-mail writer, you must take the greatest care when using copyrighted reference material.

➤ **Reword the sentence.**

Do not write: A writer who decides not to footnote source material puts his reputation at risk.

Write: Failure to footnote source material puts a writer's reputation at risk.

➤ **Use plural pronouns (they, them, their)—if you do not mind rankling a few readers.**

This option violates the long-standing rule of English grammar that a singular noun takes a singular pronoun. Along with increased concern for political correctness, however, comes a growing acceptance of the use of plural pronouns *(they, their, them)* with singular antecedent nouns.

Although traditionalists discourage the practice, it is now acceptable, in some circles, to write, for example: An e-mail user who receives a flame should give careful consideration to their attacker's motive. (But a more acceptable way to recast this particular sentence would be: An e-mail user who receives a flame should give careful consideration to the attacker's motive.)

Make It Gender Neutral

Rewrite the following two sentences, eliminating masculine pronouns and creating gender-neutral constructions.

1. Any employee who does not understand the department's e-mail policy should schedule a meeting with his supervisor.

   _____

   _____

   _____

2. The instructor must take the greatest care when he is explaining new concepts to his students.

   _____

   _____

   _____

Compare your answers with the authors' suggested responses in the Appendix.

Polishing Your

Cybermanners

Setting the Right Tone

The most effective tone for business correspondence is professional, yet conversational. How to strike that tone? Imagine you are at a professional cocktail party, attended by colleagues, supervisors, and customers. How would you speak? What type of language would you use? You would likely be conversational, yet professional, using language everyone would understand. When you write, use the same type of language and tone.

Relaxing Your Grammar

➤ **Contractions aren't bad.**

Unless you are writing a particularly formal document, go ahead and use contractions. We use contractions when we speak in business settings, and there's nothing wrong with incorporating them into business writing.

➤ **Feel free to end a sentence with a preposition.**

If you never ended a sentence with a preposition *(for, by, at, about, in, to, with, from, etc.)*, your writing would be terribly stiff, boring, and sometimes unreadable. "What is your e-mail message about?" makes considerably more sense than "About what is your e-mail message?"

➤ ***I, we*, and *you* belong in business writing.**

The purpose of most e-mail is to persuade the reader* to act in some way. Persuasion requires connection on a human level. It is hard to connect if you depersonalize your writing by eliminating all the pronouns.

➤ **And another thing...**

Go right ahead and start your sentence with a coordinating conjunction (and, or, nor, for, but, so, yet) to create a smooth transition from one sentence or thought to another.

---

*A useful reference on writing to persuade others to buy your ideas is *Writing That Sells* by Kathleen A. Begley, Ed.D., Crisp Publications.

Dodging Conversational Pitfalls

Write the way you talk is common advice in business-writing manuals. But carrying this advice too far can spell trouble. Remember, when you are communicating orally, you have the advantage of vocal variety that is absent in e-mail. The following are common pitfalls that can spoil your written messages or lessen the clarity in your correspondence.

Humor

Jokes have no place in electronic business writing. Save the humorous anecdotes for golf outings, luncheon meetings, and other in-person gatherings. Because e-mail is an impersonal medium offering none of the benefits of inflection, facial expression, or body language, electronic humor is risky business. Unless written by a professional humorist, electronic jokes are likely to fall flat or be misconstrued by the reader. At best, an attempt at humor could irritate or agitate the recipient, spelling disaster for a business relationship. Worst-case scenario: An employee's joke could trigger a workplace lawsuit.

Real-Life E-Disaster

Employee misuse of corporate e-mail can result in six-figure litigation costs and million-dollar legal settlements. In one high-profile case, Chevron Corporation in 1995 was ordered to pay female employees $2.2 million to settle a sexual harassment lawsuit stemming from inappropriate "jokes" e-mailed internally by male employees. The offenders' cyberjokes included, among other gems, "25 Reasons Why Beer is Better Than Women."[25]

Clichés

In business writing, clichés can take several forms:

➤ Compound constructions: *at that point in time* rather than *then; in the event that* vs. *if; subsequent to* for *after.*

➤ Redundant pairs: *if and when; each and every; ready and willing.*

➤ Redundant modifiers: *official e-mail from headquarters; seriously destroying our earth.*

Besides being trite and overused, clichés add unnecessary words. Do your reader and yourself a favor: Eliminate clichés.

Technical Language

If you are sending a technical e-mail document to a reader or group of readers who share your expertise, it is probably all right to use technical language. But that does not free you to write dull, unreadable messages. Even with technical material, the basics hold: Write in the active voice, eliminate unnecessary words, adhere to the mechanical rules of good writing, and write with your reader in mind.

Before you start writing in technical terms, think about hidden readers. Is there any possibility your e-mail will be read by a wider audience than you intend? If so, accommodate the nontechnical readers by including an executive summary at the beginning of your document.

Abbreviations

Use legitimate abbreviations to shorten e-mail messages only if your readers— intended and hidden—will recognize and understand them. Do not overdo it. Too many abbreviations can make a sentence hard to read.

Example:
```
I received yr. message an hr. ago and intend to act
on it ASAP. I am curious, however. Did you Cc. the
mgr. of the E Coast office as well?
```

Clarify an uncommon abbreviation on the first reference by writing it out and citing the abbreviation in parentheses. Then use the abbreviation throughout the rest of the document.

Example:
```
The findings of the International Association of
Administrative Professionals (IAAP) and ePolicy
Institute indicate growing numbers of executives
rely on administrative professionals (admins) to
ghostwrite e-mail.
```

The trend is to omit periods with abbreviations of all uppercase letters (FYI, PS). But use periods with abbreviations of all lowercase letters (e.g., mfg.). And be mindful of abbreviations that always require periods (A.M., P.M., Mr., Mrs., Dr.).

Acronyms

Electronic acronyms have found their way into e-mail messages. If you have any doubt that your intended reader will understand an acronym, do not use it.

Popular Electronic Acronyms

BCNU	be seeing you		**OBTW**	oh, by the way
BRB	be right back		**OIC**	oh, I see
BTW	by the way		**PLS**	please
CUL	see you later		**PMFJI**	pardon me for jumping in
F2F	face to face		**PRES**	presentation
FAQ	frequently asked question		**PTP**	pardon the pun
FOAF	friend of a friend		**QTY'S**	quantities
FWIW	for what it is worth		**REC'D**	received
FYA	for your amusement		**RGDS**	regards
FYEO	for your eyes only		**ROTF**	rolling on the floor
FYI	for your information		**ROTFL**	rolling on the floor laughing
GMTA	great minds think alike		**THX**	thanks
HHOK	ha-ha, only kidding		**TIA**	thanks in advance
IMHO	in my humble opinion		**TMRW**	tomorrow
IOW	in other words		**TTFN**	ta-ta for now
LOL	laughing out loud		**WB**	welcome back
MOTOS	member of the opposite sex		**WRT**	with regards to
MOTSS	member of the same sex		**WTG**	way to go
MSGS	messages		**YR**	your
NLT	no later than			

Watch Your Cyberlanguage

One of the most effective ways to reduce electronic risks also is one of the simplest. Controlling content controls risk. Thus, e-mail users should avoid language that could negatively affect business relationships, damage professional reputations, or trigger lawsuits. By using only appropriate, businesslike language in all electronic communications, you improve the overall effectiveness of your e-mail.

Appropriate e-mail content:

➤ Is free from jokes

➤ Is well-written and businesslike

➤ Is free from obscene language and sexual language

➤ Is free from racial comments

➤ Contains no harassing, menacing, negative, or defamatory comments

➤ Is free from mechanical errors and structural problems

Another way organizations can help employees follow a consistent, company-approved writing style is by developing and publishing electronic writing style guidelines, as explained in the Appendix.

Consider Technological Tools to Control Content

According to the federal Electronic Communications Privacy Act (ECPA), an employer-provided computer system is the property of the employer. Thus the employer has the right to monitor all e-mail traffic and Internet usage that take place on the company system.

Fully 62% of employers exercise their legal right to monitor employees' e-mail and Internet connections. Among those who monitor, 68% cite legal liability as the primary reason to keep an eye on employees' online activity.[26]

Employers eager to keep electronic content clean to reduce—and in some cases eliminate—e-mail risks are advised to install content security and policy management software programmed to detect, report, and/or eliminate banned content flowing into and out of your system. Visit www.epolicyinstitute.com for the authors' recommended software vendors.

Extinguishing Flames

An e-mail flame is a hostile message that is blunt, rude, insensitive, or obscene. Sending such a message is called flaming. Flames ignite quickly, as people who are upset by something they have read online send back a quick, angry reply. One flame can start an online flame war, involving numerous people transmitting angry electronic messages back and forth. Flames are unique to e-mail because the slow pace of traditional mail does not accommodate immediate, heated reaction. Before sending a flame, ask yourself the following questions:

➤ Would I say this to a person's face? If not, do not send the e-mail.

➤ Would I be embarrassed if this message were read by my supervisor or a customer, colleague, or other reader whose opinion matters to me? If so, extinguish the flame.

➤ Is it possible that the message I perceive to be a flame is actually an ill-phrased joke? If you have any doubt, assume the best.

Controlling the Urge to Flame

➤ Keep your emotions in check. Walk away from the flame, returning to the screen when you feel less heated.

➤ Write your response thoughtfully and proofread carefully before sending it. Never use obscene or abusive language in e-mail messages. The more distance you can put between a flame and your response, the less likely you will flame back.

➤ Avoid flaming in public forums. If you want to respond to a message, do so directly. Do not risk drawing others into a flame war.

Real-Life E-Disaster: The CEO's Devastating E-Mail

When the CEO of Cerner Corporation opted to use e-mail to express his displeasure about employee performance, he hoped to motivate his 400 managers to act. They acted all right, posting the CEO's angry message on Yahoo!®, where it was read by a hidden audience of 3,100 Cerner employees and also financial analysts, investors, and Yahoo subscribers. The result: Cerner's stock valuation, which was $1.5 billion the day the CEO's e-mail was sent, plummeted 22%, from $44 to $34 per share in three days.[27]

ASSESS THE FLAME

Read this excerpt of the CEO's berating e-mail. In addition to its angry tone, what other netiquette, writing, and general e-mail errors did the CEO make?

> We are getting less than 40 hours of work from a large number of our K.C.-based EMPLOYEES. The parking lot is sparsely used at 8 A.M.; likewise at 5 P.M. As managers, you either do not know what your EMPLOYEES are doing; or you do not CARE. You have created expectations on the work effort which allowed this to happen inside Cerner, creating a very unhealthy environment. In either case, you have a problem and you will fix it or I will replace you.
>
> NEVER in my career have I allowed a team which worked for me to think they had a 40-hour job. I have allowed YOU to create a culture which is permitting this. NO LONGER.
>
> You have two weeks. Tick, tock.[28]

How many e-mail mistakes can you identify?

1._____

2._____

3._____

4._____

5._____

Compare your answers with the authors' suggested responses in the Appendix.

Punctuating with Smileys and Shorthand

Unlike one-on-one meetings and telephone conversations, e-mail is a communications vehicle devoid of inflection, facial expression, and body language. To help readers interpret the e-mail writer's attitude and tone, *smileys*—also known as *emoticons*—were created as visual shorthand. Smileys, which are created with standard keyboard characters, are used by some writers to substitute for facial expressions and body language. Generally the smiley follows the punctuation mark at the end of a sentence.

The equivalent of e-mail slang, smileys should be used sparingly in personal e-mail, and not at all in business writing. Those unfamiliar with smileys will not understand them; more experienced readers will label you an e-mail novice if you overuse them. Rely on the strength of your writing—not smileys, exclamation points, or other gimmicks—to communicate your intended message in the appropriate tone.

Smiley	Emoticon Description
:-)	happy; kidding; smiling; grinning
:-(	sad; angry; chagrined

Some e-mail writers find smileys limiting, so they use electronic shorthand or a combination of smileys and acronyms to express emotions.

Shorthand	Emotion
\<g\>	grin
\<l\>	laugh
\<\>	no comment

Again, do not use electronic shorthand if you have any question about your reader's ability to understand it.

Reviewing Netiquette Guidelines

By their nature, e-mail conversations lack the warmth of face-to-face discussions and telephone calls. Couple such "coldness" with the tendency of many writers to type messages quickly and sometimes thoughtlessly, and it is easy to see the need for etiquette rules specifically related to e-mail correspondence. By adhering to these rules of *netiquette,* you can avoid problems and enhance communications with all readers—intended and hidden.

You have already learned most of these netiquette rules as you have worked through this book, so the guidelines that follow will serve as a review. Adherence to these basic rules will alleviate problems and will help cast you and your organization in a favorable light.

1   **Beware hidden readers.**
If confidentiality is an issue, do not use e-mail. It is not secure. You may intend to send an e-mail to one person. But an inaccurate keystroke or the recipient's decision to forward your message could land your e-mail on countless unintended readers' screens. Never use e-mail to communicate trade secrets, proprietary information, or any news that could damage the organization or its employees were the message to be read by an unintended reader.

2   **Write as though Mom were reading.**
People treat e-mail too casually, sending electronic messages they would never record on paper. Do not write anything you would not be comfortable saying in an elevator crowded with colleagues, customers, competitors—or Mom.

3   **Remain gender-neutral.**
You never know where your e-mail will land, so avoid sexist language. Your intended reader may be a male, but the ultimate decision-maker could be the female executive (the hidden reader) who receives a forwarded copy of your original message.

4 Keep the organization's harassment and discrimination policies in mind.

Sexual harassment and racial discrimination lawsuits have resulted from employees sending improper internal and external e-mail messages. All electronic communication should adhere to the rules set forth in the organization's harassment and discrimination policies.

5 Do not use e-mail to let off steam.

Upset or angry? Compose yourself before composing your message. Do not take the chance of sending a poorly worded message that could worsen an already difficult situation. If communication is urgently needed, ask a trusted colleague to read your document before you send it. If you have time, give yourself up to 48 hours to calm down before sending a potentially damaging message.

6 Control the urge to flame.

Flames are unique to e-mail because the slow pace of snail mail does not accommodate immediate heated reactions. Flames, and the obscene and abusive language that feed them, have no place in a business environment (or a personal setting, for that matter).

7 Respect others' time.

An in-box stuffed with recipes, jokes, health warnings, advertisements, and requests for charitable donations can be a time-consuming annoyance. Do not use the company computer system to send or forward spam. Need convincing? In some states, *spamming* (sending junk e-mail) is against the law.

8 Do not mail to the world.

Send e-mail messages only to readers with a legitimate need for your information. Mail to your group list only when it is appropriate for everyone on the list to receive the message. Do not reply to a message unless you have something to contribute. Remember, a reply to a listserv sender is a reply to every subscriber on the list.

9 **Copy with care.**
Sending a carbon copy *(Cc)* or blind carbon copy *(Bcc)* to a recipient who does not need to read your message wastes everyone's time. As a rule, address your message to the person you want to motivate to act, and send carbon copies strictly as a courtesy. Carbon copy recipients are not required to reply to messages, so do not get upset when a response is not forthcoming.

10 **Do not oversell your message.**
Just because you have the ability to mark messages *urgent* does not mean you should. Reserve the urgent classification for messages that demand immediate action.

11 **Ask permission to forward material.**
Do you subscribe to an *e-zine,* or electronic newsletter, that would interest an associate or customer? Do not hit *Forward* without asking permission of the original sender. Otherwise you may be in violation of copyright law.

12 **Keep your editorial comments to yourself.**
Just as few speakers appreciate having their grammar corrected publicly by co-workers, few e-mail writers would enjoy receiving an unsolicited critique of their electronic writing.

13 **Treat others as you would have them treat you.**
If you receive someone else's e-mail by mistake, do not trash it. Hit *Reply* to direct it back to the sender, along with a brief note about the mix-up.

14 **Consider e-mail's limitations.**
E-mail may be the best way to deliver news fast, but it is not necessarily the best route to a quick reply. Your reader is under no obligation to check incoming messages regularly, if at all. And it is inappropriate to send a follow-up message demanding to know why a recipient has not responded to your message. For an immediate response to a pressing issue, pick up the phone or schedule a face-to-face meeting.

Put Netiquette into Practice

After ordering a baby crib from an online furniture retailer, a new mother e-mailed the company's customer service department to express displeasure over slow delivery. But the customer service department's reply was not the answer the buyer was hoping for. How many netiquette errors can you identify? (Yes, this is a real message!)

Dear Customer:

We got your feedback on doing business with our company. Obviously you never read the attached note we sent you the day after we received your order!!!!

Also, our site says we will process your order withing 2-3 days of receiving it, not drop it at your door. Further, our order process confirmation says allow upto 5 business days in transit while in the hands of the ground transportation service.

We did everything we said we would do for you. Problem is you do not read.

Please do not return to us as a customer, since you are exactly the type we do not want.

Our rating of you as a customer is: Ignorant and enjoys it.

Sincerely,

Customer Service

CONTINUED

Netiquette Errors:

1._____

2._____

3._____

4._____

5._____

6._____

Draft a more appropriate e-mail response to the customer's complaint.

_____

_____

_____

_____

_____

_____

_____

_____

_____

_____

_____

_____

Compare your answers with the authors' suggested responses in the Appendix.

Netiquette Guidelines for Managers

Executives and managers should adhere to the same basic rules of netiquette as outlined in the preceding section. A handful of additional netiquette considerations apply also to those who supervise employees.

1 **Regularly remind employees that the organization has the right to monitor employee e-mail transmissions.**
Do not allow employees to assume they can expect privacy from the organization's computer assets.

2 **Enforce the organization's e-mail policy consistently.**
If, for example, the e-mail policy prohibits the downloading of attachments, adhere to that prohibition yourself. Do not allow yourself rights that other employees cannot enjoy equally.

If the organization's e-policy states that employees will be terminated for sending e-mail messages that violate the organization's sexual harassment policy, managers must follow through by firing violators. The only way the organization's e-mail policy will be effective at reducing liability risks is through consistent enforcement.

3 **Be realistic about the company's personal-use policy.**
More than 70% of employers allow limited, approved personal e-mail use.[29] E-mail may be the only means for some employees to keep in touch with partners and immediate family during working hours. Working parents who are prohibited from communicating with family members via e-mail may decide to look for a more family-friendly employer.

4 **Never use e-mail to fire employees or deliver bad news.**
Whether your objective is to terminate an employee or notify a department head of budgetary cutbacks, demonstrate respect for your employees by delivering bad news in person. A one-on-one meeting will give the employee the opportunity to ask questions and absorb the shock of bad news. And, should a wrongful termination lawsuit follow, personal notification will cast management in a better light than electronic notification would.

5 **Do not use e-mail to discuss an employee's performance with others.**

As a manager, you are not required to like every employee personally. But you are obligated to treat each worker with professional courtesy. If you need to discuss an employee's professional shortcomings with the human resources director or instruct a department head to terminate an employee who is not working out, do so in person and behind closed doors.

E-mail is fraught with too many dangers for sensitive or confidential communication. You could strike your group-list key accidentally, sending negative comments about an employee's work to everyone in the organization. You could type in the address of the employee in question, rather than the human resources director, and alert the employee (and the employee's lawyer) to your feelings and comments.

Worst case scenario: If the employee in question were to file a workplace lawsuit, alleging a hostile work environment or wrongful termination, your electronic discussion with the human resources director could come back to haunt the company as a whole. E-mail messages, like written performance reviews and other documents, can be subject to discovery and subpoena in litigation. In a trial, your e-mail messages about this employee could be used as evidence against the organization.

 Do not rely on e-mail to the exclusion of personal contact.

To varying degrees, your employees, customers, and suppliers all crave human interaction. Although some people may be content to communicate electronically nearly 100% of the time, others may feel slighted or unappreciated unless you maintain ongoing personal contact. Even in the age of e-mail, relationship skills remain at the heart of long-term business success. Supplement your e-mail communication by holding regular meetings with your staff, customers, and important suppliers.

7 **Avoid e-mail if there is any chance your message will be misunderstood.**
If your message is complex, technical, or otherwise in any danger of being misinterpreted, opt for a telephone call or a personal meeting instead of e-mail.

8 **Do not rely solely on e-mail to communicate e-mail policy to employees.**
Create a sense of policy ownership among employees by holding e-policy training sessions. Explain why the company has created the e-mail policy and what you and the rest of the management team expect from the staff. Create an environment in which employees feel free to ask questions about the organization's electronic policy.

Formatting Your
E-Mail Message

Selecting Format Settings

Newer e-mail packages allow seemingly endless choices of attention-getting fonts, colors, margins, bullets, and other graphic devices and formatting options. But be aware that your ability to send e-mail messages that incorporate unusual elements is only as good as your reader's e-mail software. Remember, readability is the name of the game. If your message is not legible, the recipient may not have the patience to wade through it, no matter how important. Thus, for business purposes especially, it is best to stick with tried-and-true format settings. Otherwise, if your reader's e-mail software is incompatible with yours, the results can be disastrous.

Here are some guidelines for making your documents easy to read.

1. Maintain appropriate margins

2. Choose the right font

3. Select the appropriate colors

Maintain Appropriate Margins

What you see on your screen may not be what your readers see. If their computer systems or e-mail packages are different from yours, your line lengths can cause an annoying text-wrap effect on their screens, which can throw off special formatting effects you may have incorporated. To be safe, keep your lines to 55 or 60 characters, including spaces. Exaggerate any indentation you use to make sure it "catches" on your readers' screens.

Choose the Right Font

Few things are harder to read than e-mail composed with unusual type or exceptionally large or small characters. If your subject is business-related, create a polished, professional look by using a standard typeface such as Times New Roman, Courier, or Arial. And stick with the 10-point to 12-point font sizes most readers are comfortable with:

10-point Times New Roman

11-point Courier

12-point Arial

For headings or other special elements within your e-mail, a larger font size delivers more impact, but should be used sparingly.

If your topic is personal, you can inject personality into your writing by using a font such as Bellevue, Hobo, or Goudy Handtooled to communicate a casual tone:

10-point Bellevue

11-point Hobo

12-point Goudy Handtooled

A good typeface policy for all e-mail: not too small, not too large, not too ornate.

Select Appropriate Colors

Your e-mail package may give you the option of changing the background or font colors of your message. Resist the urge to exercise this option. Although a purple background with lime-green letters might create an interesting look, it also may undercut your credibility. For business correspondence, use a neutral or light background with dark letters. Unusual screen colors can be hard to read, and they can detract from or conflict with the tone of your communication.

Enhancing Readability

Because of the high volume of e-mails that many people receive every day, you need to do everything possible to make your message stand out for its readability.

E-mail messages are most effective if kept short. But if you must send a lengthy message, forecast the structure. On your readers' first screen, summarize your message and then indicate what is to come with a listing of your section headings. You can ease reading long passages by using the same devices you see in the newspaper:

➤ Occasional all caps, bolds, and underlining

➤ Headings

➤ Lists

➤ White space

➤ Indentation

Resisting the Urge to Use All Upper- or Lowercase Letters

To draw attention to on-screen messages, some e-mail writers use all capital letters. Bad idea. A message written in all uppercase letters is more difficult to read than one written in standard style. The human eye is used to reading a mixture of uppercase and lowercase letters. When you draft e-mail in all uppercase letters, you run the risk of slowing down—and annoying—your reader. Moreover, using all uppercase often comes across as shouting.

For the same reason—readability—resist the urge to write e-mail messages in all lowercase letters, which can come across as juvenile or cutesy. It may be quicker to write in all caps or all lowercase, but the result will be more difficult to read and less professional.

A Readability Quiz

Test your reaction to the following passage, written in three styles: all capitals, all lowercase letters, and the standard mixture of uppercase and lowercase. Which do you find most readable?

1. THE WALL STREET JOURNAL REPORTS THE AVERAGE OFFICE WORKER SPENDS 49 MINUTES ON E-MAIL EACH DAY, WHILE TOP MANAGEMENT DEVOTES A WHOPPING FOUR HOURS A DAY TO E-MAIL.[30]

2. the wall street journal reports the average office worker spends 49 minutes on e-mail each day, while top management devotes a whopping four hours a day to e-mail.

3. The Wall Street Journal reports the average office worker spends 49 minutes on e-mail each day, while top management devotes a whopping four hours a day to e-mail.

Emphasizing Electronic Text

Because of incompatibility problems among e-mail software packages, electronic writers have adopted common conventions for italicizing and underlining text. Use these electronic symbols judiciously, however, because confusion can result if your reader is unfamiliar with them.

To Italicize: Type an asterisk (*) on each side of the word or phrase to be italicized. For example, to italicize the word *write*, surround it with asterisks: The movie star didn't actually *write* his autobiography; he told his story to a ghostwriter.

To Underline: Add the underscore character before and after the copy to be underlined. For example, to underline The American Heritage Dictionary, introduce and follow it with the underscore character: Every e-mail writer should own a good, up-to-date dictionary such as _The American Heritage Dictionary_.

Arranging Text into Vertical Lists

Arranging text into bulleted or numbered vertical lists, as appropriate, gives your document a quick-read quality that long narratives cannot. Some e-mail programs include the option of formatting lists with bullets, but if not, you may substitute an asterisk (*) or double hyphens (--). Numbered vertical lists are generally used only for a sequence of steps. Either way, apply the following tips to maximize the effectiveness of such lists:

> ➤ Be consistent. If your list starts with an asterisk, then each item in the list should start with one.

> ➤ Write complete sentences or sentence fragments, but be consistent throughout the list.

> ➤ Begin each item in the list with a capital letter.

> ➤ Keep each line short.

> ➤ Indent the list, if desired, to call more attention to it.

> ➤ Add even more emphasis to each point by double-spacing and leaving plenty of white space around the list.

Do not be afraid of white space. An extra line or two before and after an important section—in a list or within a paragraph—adds impact and enhances readability.

As an alternative to vertical lists, you can construct numbered lists within sentences and paragraphs. This approach saves space while enhancing readability.

Example: Vertical lists are most effective when the writer: (1) keeps each line short; (2) indents for maximum readability; and (3) creates white space by double-spacing.

Sending Attachments with Care

Most e-mail messages will be contained on one screen, though some topics warrant extra space. If the message would go on for many screens, or if you need to incorporate letterhead, charts, or graphics into your message, attach a separate document. The attachment feature, available on most e-mail software, enables you to attach, or add, documents that have been created in separate files. Attachment software expands the capabilities of e-mail, allowing the writer to deliver longer, more comprehensive documents, including word processing, spreadsheets, charts, and graphics.

Before attaching a document, however, consider its appropriateness.

> ➤ **Can your reader's e-mail system accommodate your attachment?** Before attaching a document to your e-mail message, consider the software your reader is using. When in doubt, send a quick e-mail or call your recipient. A little effort before writing will save time and eliminate frustration later.

> ➤ **Is the recipient allowed to open attachments?** To block viruses and save bandwidth, some organizations ban the opening of attachments altogether. Check to make sure your reader's e-mail policy allows the opening of attachments before you send.

> ➤ **Generate reader interest in the attachment.** Use your e-mail message to provide a brief description of the attachment and sell the reader on its merits. Resist the temptation to write a detailed message about the attachment.

> ➤ **Do not send an attachment when a brief message will do.** Before attaching a document, consider its value. If a brief e-mail message will do the job, do not bother attaching a file.

> ➤ **Compress extremely large files.** Attaching extremely large documents—databases, graphics, spreadsheets—can be a problem. As an alternative, consider using a compression program to reduce the size of large attachments, but make sure your recipient has the capability to decompress the file.

> ➤ **Attach first, write second.** Have you ever received an e-mail that referenced a nonexisting attachment? Most of us have, or we have sent a note and forgotten to attach a promised document. Make it a point to add your attachment first—before you compose your note.

Attaching Files Step-By-Step

Although e-mail packages vary, attaching files generally is a four-step process:

Step 1: Select the attachment option on your screen. It may appear as the word *Attach* or as an icon symbolizing an attachment. Check your software manual if you are unclear about your system's icon.

Step 2: Select the document to be attached from the appropriate folder.

Step 3: Repeat the process if you are attaching multiple documents.

Step 4: After you confirm your selection, your original e-mail message window will reappear, indicating the document(s) attached.

For specific instructions on how to attach documents to your e-mail, refer to your e-mail software's *Help* menu.

Note: It is easy to get sidetracked while writing the message and forget to attach the referenced document. Avoid this problem by attaching the file first, then composing your message.

Battling Electronic Viruses

Whenever you send or receive e-mail, you risk catching and spreading a computer virus. Some viruses are merely irritating, not destructive. Other viruses, sent with malicious intent, are more harmful. A destructive virus can erase files from your disk, impede system processing, and transfer itself from one computer to another.

E-mail attachments are the most common form of virus transportation. If you open an infected word-processing document, spreadsheet, or other attachment, there is a good chance of catching the bug.

The best medicine is preventive: Never open an attachment unless you know the sender. (Of course, the sender may not know a file is infected.) Be sure to install the latest virus detection software to automatically check all incoming e-mail for viruses and eliminate problems before they damage your computer or system.

Managing E-Mail

Overload

Controlling Your In-Box Clutter

Are you drowning in e-mail? You are not alone. According to research firm International Data Corp., e-mail is growing at a rate of 66% annually, with 1.4 trillion e-mail messages sent from North American businesses in 2001, up from 40 billion in 1995.[31]

E-mail has become the most common way for business people to communicate with internal and external audiences. An Accountemps poll indicated that 37% of executives say they spend one to two hours a day reading and sending e-mail.[32] Keeping e-mail under control takes a careful balance of common sense, organizational skills, and e-mail policy, as suggested in the following strategies:

1 Do not feel obliged to read and respond to every message.
You are under no obligation to read or reply to every e-mail message that lands in your mailbox. You determine when to respond to messages. If a message is truly important, the sender, not the receiver, should follow up with a phone call to make sure the message was received and that a timely response is forthcoming.

2 Assign your administrative professional the role of electronic gatekeeper.
Managers are increasingly relying on administrative professionals to help manage their electronic burden. According to a survey conducted by the International Association of Administrative Professionals (IAAP) and The ePolicy Institute, 26% of admins screen executives' incoming e-mail; 29% are authorized to delete e-mail addressed to the executive; and 43% ghostwrite e-mail responses under their executives' names.[33]

3 Whittle down your mail.
Ignore and delete what you can. Read and respond only to legitimate mail. Before you start opening mail:

➤ Do a quick subject line scan and delete obvious sales pitches or spam. Do not take time to open or read this mail. (Reducing spam intake is covered later in this chapter.)

➤ Delete all messages from strangers or senders with odd addresses.

➤ Empty your delete folder regularly. Messages will sit in your electronic recycle bin forever unless you take steps to empty it.

Manage your time wisely.

➤ Scan the first three sentences for the meat of the message. Reply immediately to succinct, to-the-point messages. Set aside wordy missives for later.

➤ Rank your e-mail. Read and respond to high-priority and business-related messages first. Depending upon your organization's e-mail policy, personal correspondence—if it is permitted at all—should be saved for breaks, downtime, or reading at home.

➤ Do not waste time replying to copies and blind carbon copies unless your commentary is critical.

File and archive saved e-mail.

To save e-mail messages on your computer without cluttering your inbox, file or archive them.

Filing is the organizing of active messages that you want to save on your computer for convenient access. Sort mail by category and create files into which you can divert time-consuming mail, such as newsletters and listserv e-mail, for later review.

Archiving is the storing of older messages that no longer belong on your computer but that you may want access to later.

Filing e-mail is as simple as creating and labeling document folders to store individual messages. Depending on your e-mail package, you probably will take the following steps when filing:

1. Select the document you wish to file.

2. Select the folder in which you want to keep the document.

3. Give your document a file name.

4. Click on *Save*.

It is a good idea to conduct an annual review of all the documents in your folders. Archive those documents that you no longer need on your computer but are not ready to delete.

To archive a document, save the folder or document to a CD or diskette, then delete the files from your computer. Using file compression software will make the files easier to manage. Store the archive discs in a safe place, off-site if they are particularly valuable.

Remember to back up your document folders regularly. All the e-mail management in the world will not matter if you cannot recover data in an emergency.

Establish e-mail guidelines for your colleagues and staff.

Managers may want to set guidelines for their departments or work teams to help manage e-mail flow. For example:

➤ Limit e-mail to three sentences. If you cannot say it in three sentences, make a call or schedule a face-to-face meeting.

➤ Do not send e-mail to colleagues who are working next door, on the same floor, or even in the same building.

➤ Do not use e-mail to schedule lunch or internal meetings.

Maintain your perspective.

With the advent of portable e-mail devices and e-mail pagers, it is tempting to be connected around the clock. Resist that temptation by establishing clear boundaries for e-communication. Set aside a specific amount of time each day for reading, writing, and responding to e-mail. Handle business correspondence at work and save personal e-mail for home, or risk potential disciplinary action or termination for violating your organization's e-mail policy.

Reducing Spam Intake

As an e-mail user, you probably receive plenty of spam. Electronic junk mail includes primarily advertisements, get-rich-quick schemes, and adult-oriented material. Try the following spam-busting techniques to reduce your intake of these annoying messages.

➤ Never reply to spam. If you are on the receiving end of a spam mailing, do not reply to the *unsubscribe* option. Often such a reply accomplishes the opposite. Your reply confirms your e-mail address and may encourage the sender to sell your address to other spammers. Replying to spam also can be a waste of time because senders sometimes use one-time-only addresses to blast the spam into cyberspace. Your irate reply could land nowhere. So why bother?

➤ Consider simply deleting unsolicited messages. A simple solution, deleting junk e-mail is the easiest, most effective way to control spam.

➤ When sending e-mail messages to recipients you do not know, ask that your address not be forwarded or sold.

➤ Buy software to filter out unwanted messages. Some filtering programs are based on key words and phrases. Add "get rich quick" to your filter list, and messages containing that phrase will be deleted. Other filtering programs send unwanted messages to a dedicated folder, which you periodically delete without reading. The downside to this approach is that legitimate messages could slip through and be deleted along with the junk.

➤ For confidential messages, use encryption software that scrambles contents, making messages indecipherable to all but the intended recipient.

Organization-Wide E-Mail Management

1 Establish and enforce a written e-mail policy.

Help employees manage their e-mail by establishing clear guidelines for the appropriate use of the organization's e-mail system, as outlined in the next section. Put teeth in your e-mail policy by enforcing it consistently, regardless of the violator's rank or tenure. For further information, visit the authors' Web site, www.epolicyinstitute.com.

2 Establish clear guidelines for business and personal e-mail use.

To limit employees' personal use of the company e-mail system, establish clear guidelines for business and personal use. Use your written policy to notify employees that the organization's e-mail system is provided for business use. If you permit personal use of the company system, be sure to spell out exactly what type and how much personal e-mail management authorizes. In the United States, employers handle personal e-mail use in five ways[34]:

➤ 39% allow full and unrestricted personal use of office e-mail

➤ 24% ban all personal use of office e-mail

➤ 21% allow full personal use with prior management approval

➤ 7% permit personal use for emergencies only

➤ 4% allow communication only with immediate family

Employers who allow personal e-mail place the following time restrictions on employees:

➤ 10% allow personal use of the e-mail system only during non-business hours

➤ 7% set specific time duration limits

➤ 2% have time limits during business hours only

3 Educate employees about e-mail use and electronic time management.

➤ Explain when e-mail should be used and when it should be avoided

➤ Address e-mail netiquette for employees and managers

➤ Discuss productivity concerns and other electronic risks

4 Establish a document retention and deletion strategy.

Half of the United States' largest corporations and national associations lack a formal policy for naming, archiving, or purging electronic files.[35] Critical to effective e-mail management is establishing a document retention and deletion policy that spells out for employees how to categorize files, where to store files, and when and how to destroy files. If there is a workplace lawsuit, your document retention and deletion policy will play a critical, and potentially costly, role. Because there is no one-size-fits-all retention and deletion policy that works for all organizations, employers should consult with a legal expert experienced with electronic document management.

5 Control what you can centrally.

Assign limited e-mail space on your file server. Reduce mailbox size, and employees who tend to over-save mail will simply run out of room. Install software that allows your e-mail administrator to empty employees' delete folders automatically.

6 Install content security and policy management software.

Reduce e-mail overload with filtering software designed to get the spam out of your system. Install policy management and content security software to ensure employees are complying with written e-mail policy and using your system and their time appropriately and productively. For the authors' recommended software vendors, visit www.epolicyinstitute.com

DEVISE YOUR OWN E-STRATEGIES

Create an e-mail management strategy for you and your organization. List up to 10 action steps you can take to help manage your e-mail flow and that of your organization as a whole.

Personal E-Mail Management Action Steps:

1._____

2._____

3._____

4._____

5._____

6._____

7._____

8._____

9._____

10._____

Organizational E-Mail Management Action Steps:

1._____

2._____

3._____

4._____

5._____

6._____

7._____

8._____

9._____

10._____

Compare your answers with the authors' suggested responses in the Appendix.

Devising an E-Mail Policy for Your Organization

Regardless of industry type or number of employees, all organizations that allow employees access to the e-mail system should have a written policy in place. The following guidelines will help you devise a policy that suits your organization.

➤ Establish a comprehensive written e-mail policy for your organization and enforce it equally with officers, managers, supervisors, and staff.

➤ Communicate that the organization's e-mail system is to be used as a business communications tool. Provide clear guidance on what is, and is not, considered appropriate electronic business communication.

➤ Bear in mind that some personal use of your organization's e-mail system may be warranted. American workers today put in more on-the-job hours than at any other time in history. For employees who leave the house before dawn and do not return until well past dark, e-mail may be the most efficient and effective way to stay in touch with family members. For the sake of employee morale and retention, savvy employers generally are willing to accommodate their employees' need to check in electronically with partners and immediate family. Let your employees know where you stand on this issue, and how much personal use (if any) is acceptable.

➤ Incorporate an overview of your organization's discrimination and sexual harassment policies within your e-mail policy. Because of the relaxed, informal nature of e-mail, some employees will put in writing comments they never would say aloud. Make sure employees understand that, regardless of how it is transmitted, inappropriate comments are off-limits. All it takes is one offensive e-mail message to land you on the wrong side of an expensive, protracted workplace lawsuit.

➤ Review your written e-mail policy with every employee. New hires and long-time employees, managers and supervisors, full-time professionals and part-time staff, telecommuters and temporary employees, independent contractors and freelancers, should all be informed of your e-mail policy. Have each employee sign and date a copy of the policy to confirm they have read, understood, and agree to comply with it. Use e-mail messages, along with the company's intranet, to remind employees of the e-mail policy and management's commitment to enforcing it.

➤ Incorporate your written e-mail policy into your organization's employee handbook and new-hire orientation materials. Make sure the organization's human resources director understands the importance of reviewing the e-mail policy with every new employee.

➤ Address ownership issues and privacy expectations. Let employees know that the contents of the e-mail system, including passwords, belong to the organization, not the individual user. If management monitors and reads employee e-mail, say so. Make sure employees understand that their e-mail can, and will, be read at any time without notice to or permission of the employee. If there is any chance you may want to monitor employees' home computers, make that clear as well.

➤ Support your e-mail policy with e-writing guidelines and cyberlanguage policies designed to reduce risks by controlling content.

➤ Establish netiquette policies for e-mail senders and receivers, managers and staff.

➤ Install software to monitor and filter e-mail traveling into and out of your system.

➤ Educate employees about the "whys" behind your e-mail policies. Make employees aware of electronic risks and the repercussions they will face for violating e-mail policy.

➤ If you do business or operate facilities abroad, include in your e-mail policy a discussion about effective international e-communication.

➤ Do not allow employees to dismiss the organization's e-mail policy as insignificant or unenforceable. Inform employees that their e-mail transmissions will be monitored. Stress that e-mail policy violators will face disciplinary action that may include termination. Let employees know you mean business by enforcing your e-mail policy consistently, regardless of the offender's rank or tenure with the company.

For detailed information about the development and implementation of written e-mail policies, see *The ePolicy Handbook* by Nancy Flynn. Available online at the author's Web site, www.epolicyinstitute.com.

Using a Sample E-Mail Policy as a Guide

(Insert Organization's Name) E-Mail Policy

(Organization) is pleased to make e-mail access available to authorized employees. Created as a business tool to help (Organization) employees serve customers, communicate with suppliers, streamline internal communications, and reduce unnecessary paperwork, the e-mail system is intended primarily for business purposes. Personal use of (Organization's) e-mail system is restricted to the terms outlined as follows. The e-mail system is the property of (Organization). Employees accessing (Organization's) e-mail system are required to adhere to the following policy and procedures. Violation of (Organization's) e-mail policy may result in disciplinary action, up to and including termination.

1. All communications and information transmitted, received, or archived in (Organization's) computer system belong to the company. The federal Electronic Communications Privacy Act (ECPA) gives management the right to access and review all employee e-mail messages transmitted or received via the organization's computer system. (Organization) intends to exercise our legal right to monitor employees' e-mail activity. When it comes to e-mail, employees should have no expectation of privacy. Be aware that management may access and monitor e-mail at any time for any reason without notice.

2. The e-mail system is reserved primarily for business use. Only under the following circumstances may employees use (Organization's) e-mail system for personal reasons:

   a) Communication with partners and immediate family is permitted but must be limited to no more than 15 minutes a day during business hours. Employees also are free to e-mail partners and immediate family during the lunch hour and other authorized break times.

   b) Personal e-mail communication that exceeds the time limits outlined in point 2a and/or that is conducted between the employee and an individual other than a partner or immediate family member is prohibited unless authorized by (Organization's) human resources manager.

c) The use of (Organization's) e-mail system to solicit for any purpose, campaign for a political candidate, espouse political views, promote a religious cause, and/or advertise the sale of merchandise is strictly prohibited without the prior approval of the chief information officer.

3. E-mail passwords are the property of (Organization). Employees are required to provide the chief information officer with current passwords. Only authorized personnel are permitted to use passwords to access another employee's e-mail without consent. Misuse of passwords, the sharing of passwords with nonemployees, and/or the unauthorized use of another employee's password will result in disciplinary action, up to and including termination.

4. Privacy does not exist in cyberspace. Confidential or personal information never should be sent via e-mail without the understanding that it can be intercepted. This includes the transmission of customer financial information, social security numbers, employee health records, proprietary data and trade secrets, and/or other confidential material. When sending confidential material (or any messages for that matter), employees should use extreme caution to ensure the intended recipient's e-mail address is correct.

5. Employees must exercise sound judgment and common sense when distributing e-mail messages. Client-related messages should be carefully guarded and protected. Employees must also abide by copyright laws, ethics rules, and other applicable laws. Employees should send blind carbon copies cautiously to ensure addressees' privacy is not violated by inadvertently sending carbon copies.

6. E-mail usage must conform to (Organization's) harassment and discrimination policies. Messages containing defamatory, obscene, menacing, threatening, offensive, harassing, or otherwise objectionable and/or inappropriate statements—and/or messages that disclose personal information without authorization—are prohibited. If employees

receive such a prohibited, unsolicited message, they must not forward it, but notify their supervisor and/or the chief information officer about the message, then delete the message as instructed by management.

7. E-mail messages should be treated as formal business documents, written in accord with (Organization's) Electronic Writing Style and Netiquette Guidelines. Style, spelling, grammar, and punctuation should be appropriate and accurate, and the rules of netiquette must be adhered to.

8. Employees are prohibited from sending jokes via e-mail. Jokes, which often contain objectionable material, are easily misconstrued when communicated electronically.

9. Employees are prohibited from sending organization-wide e-mail messages to all employees without approval from the chief information officer. In addition, employees are prohibited from requesting e-mail replies to organization-wide e-mail without the permission of the chief information officer.

10. Employees may not waste (Organization's) computer resources or colleagues' time. Employees should send e-mail messages and copies only to those with a legitimate need to read the message. Chain messages and executable graphics should be deleted, not forwarded, because they can overload the system.

11. Only the chief information officer and/or systems administrator may generate public mail distribution lists.

12. Employees are responsible for knowing and adhering to (Organization's) e-mail retention and deletion policies.

13. Misuse and/or abuse of (Organization's) electronic assets (wasting productive time online, copying or downloading copyrighted materials, visiting inappropriate sites, sending inappropriate or abusive e-mail messages, etc.) will result in disciplinary action, up to and including termination.

Employee Acknowledgment

Note: If you have questions or concerns about (Organization's) E-Mail Policy, contact the chief information officer and/or human resources director (e-mail addresses and phone numbers) before signing this agreement.

I have read (Organization's) E-Mail Policy and agree to abide by it. I understand violation of any of the above terms may result in discipline, up to and including my termination.

_____   _____   _____

Employee Name (Printed)   Employee Signature   Date

A P P E N D I X

Drafting Electronic Writing Style Guidelines for Your Organization[36]

Establishing company-wide electronic writing style guidelines helps streamline the electronic writing process for employees while ensuring the creation of e-mail messages that reflect the organization's overall professionalism and credibility. Consider incorporating the following points into your organization's e-style sheet:

1 **Salutations**

Does your organization have a policy governing the way that external readers are addressed? Do you prefer e-mail writers address customers, clients, and other nonemployees as *Mr., Ms., Dr., Professor,* and the like, or are first names allowed? If *Mr.* and *Ms.* are required at first, at what point in the business relationship may employees switch to the reader's first name?

If you have not formally addressed salutations elsewhere, do so in your e-writing policy. This minor but potentially thorny issue can slow down the writing process for employees who just cannot decide how to address an e-mail recipient.

2 **Signatures**

Have you established rules for message sign-off? Giving employees a choice of three standard closes (*Sincerely, Cordially,* and *Best Regards,* for example) will speed the writing process and eliminate the possibility of employees' wrapping up business correspondence with quirky signature statements.

3 **Capitalization**

Is there consistency within your organization on capitalization? How do your employees handle the capitalizing of job titles, departments, job functions, and so on? Are the words *Company* and *Organization* to be capitalized? Use your e-writing policy to let employees know what words are to be capitalized, when.

Names

Do employees consistently refer to your organization by the same name? If not, is there a chance of creating confusion among readers? Consider adopting a policy so that, on the first reference, the company name is spelled out in full (The ePolicy Institute™); then on every subsequent reference, a company-approved shortened version of the name may be used (ePolicy Institute). Such a naming guideline prevents employees from using the considerably less formal and potentially confusing *ePolicy,* while saving them the tedium of spelling out the company name in full throughout their e-mail.

Technical Terms and Professional Jargon

The language of a particular industry's insiders is best restricted to the intranet and other internal communications. A jargon-laden message that is forwarded to a nontechnical recipient or lands on the screen of a hidden reader could create confusion and lessen the reader's acceptance of future messages from the writer in question.

Spellings

Does your organization or industry regularly use words that have optional spellings (theatre or theater, catalogue or catalog, disc or disk, etc.)? Simplify life for your employees by developing a corporate vocabulary list, complete with preferred spellings.

Working Around Oddities

In Internet commerce, company names sometimes begin with lowercase letters. If that is so for your company or clients, make accommodations in your employee writing guidelines. For example, because sentences must begin with a capital letter, instruct employees to rewrite sentences in which a lowercase company name appears as the first word. Consider the sentence, "www.epolicyinstitute.com, the leading online source of e-mail writing, e-mail management, and e-policy training tools and services, offers visitors a wealth of free content." This sentence can be reworked easily to: "The nation's leading online source of e-mail writing, e-mail management, and e-policy training tools and services, www.epolicyinstitute.com offers visitors a wealth of free content."

Directory of E-Mail Hardware

E-mail is available on a variety of hardware devices. Here is a quick overview of the tools you can use to send and receive electronic messages.

Desktop/Network E-Mail

The vast majority of e-mail is sent and received on desktop or laptop computers. The e-mail software resides either on the computer itself or in the network to which the computer is attached.

Advantages:

➤ Robust software provides a full range of features and functions

➤ Plentiful storage for your e-mail messages

➤ Off-line access to your e-mail. You do not have to be connected to your e-mail provider to compose new messages or read replies.

Disadvantages:

➤ Limited mobility. You must use your desktop/laptop computer or be signed on to your network to access the software.

Web E-Mail

Increasingly Internet service providers and Web sites are offering e-mail services to subscribers and visitors. Simply register once, then access your e-mail at any time from any computer connected to the Internet.

Advantages:

➤ Freedom of movement. You do not have to be logged on to your own computer to send and receive e-mail.

Disadvantages:

➤ Limited features and functions compared to desktop e-mail software

➤ Limited storage space for messages

➤ No off-line access to your e-mail

➤ Access to attachments you might want to send is limited to the computer or network you are using at the time

Instant Messaging

Instant messaging is akin to making an online phone call. With the Internet and an instant messaging software program, you can communicate with anyone who is logged on at the same time.

Advantages:

➤ The instant give-and-take associated with phone chat. Unlike standard e-mail—which involves composing and sending messages, then waiting for replies—instant messaging takes place in real time.

Disadvantages:

➤ Incompatibility issues between competing instant messaging software providers

➤ Lack of the basic e-mail features and functions available on most desktop or Web e-mail programs.

Personal Digital Assistants (PDAs)

PDAs provide convenient access to your calendar, contact list, and note pad. If your PDA is Web-enabled with a wireless modem, you can also send and receive e-mail.

Advantages:

➤ Portability. Slip your PDA into your pocket or briefcase and off you go.

➤ Off-line access to e-mail received and messages you are composing.

➤ The ability to sync your PDA to your desktop computer, so e-mail can be transferred between hardware devices.

Disadvantages:

➤ Inconsistent coverage. If you are out of cell phone range, you are probably out of range to transmit and receive wireless e-mail messages.

➤ Although manufacturers are beginning to offer keypads that enhance ease of use, many PDAs have small keypads while others have no keypad at all. To write messages, you write or tap letters on the screen with a stylus or your thumb.

Two-Way Text Pagers

The traditional one-way pager has been updated to allow you to send and receive e-mail messages.

Advantages:

➤ Portability—just clip it and go

➤ Small and lightweight

Disadvantages:

➤ Inconsistent coverage—unlike one-way pagers (which have great coverage), the coverage for two-way pagers is about the same as a cell phone

➤ Small keypads—most people learn to type with their thumbs

➤ Limited message size—usually in the range of 100 to 400 characters

Cell Phones

Many cell phones also allow you to send and receive e-mail.

Advantages:

➤ Portability and convenience—one device handles phone and text messages

Disadvantages:

➤ Coverage can be spotty outside of metro areas

➤ Small keypads

➤ Limited message size

Which Device Is Right for You?

To answer this question, you will need to evaluate your electronic messaging needs. When you need to send more formal correspondence, you will probably want to use desktop, Web e-mail, or perhaps a PDA. For less formal messages (akin to a phone call), a PDA, instant messaging, cell phone, or two-way e-mail pager will probably do the trick.

Mind Your Electronic Manners

Although portable e-mail devices and e-mail pagers offer round-the-clock connection, not everyone is interested in being online 24/7. Use a PDA or e-mail pager to send messages instantly, but do not expect an immediate reply. Unless your organization's e-mail policy requires employees to check and respond to e-mail seven days a week at specific intervals, your recipient is under no obligation to open, read, or reply to e-mail that arrives after business hours, if at all. The same holds true for clients, prospects, and suppliers.

Author's Suggested Responses

Part 2: Composing Your E-Mail Message

Draft a Subject Line (Page 23)

Effective six-word subject lines include:

1. Attend Mandatory E-Mail Policy Meeting

2. Improve Staff Productivity. Results Guaranteed.

Strengthen the Lead (Page 27)

The three most important sentences are:

1. Effective today, Jane has been named communications chief for the State Health Department.

2. All supervisors, managers, and staff will begin reporting to Jane immediately.

3. Please plan to attend tomorrow's 7 A.M. staff meeting to learn more about Jane's promotion and her plans for the department.

The following is a message you might write using the three lead sentences:

Effective immediately, Jane Tomm has been named communications chief for the State Health Department. All employees will now report to Jane. Please attend tomorrow's 7 A.M. staff meeting to learn more about Jane's promotion and her plans for the department. For those who are unfamiliar with Jane, she is a 12-year state employee and an integral member of the Health Department's public relations team, where she served first as a public information officer, then as manager of special projects. A graduate of State University, with a master's in journalism and a bachelor's in English, Jane has published two books of children's fiction and is a volunteer tutor with the city schools, teaching writing skills to high school students.

Part 3: Keys to Effective E-Mail

Rewrite for Readability (Page 37)

In the following sentences, the main points are underlined, and brackets enclose needless words and phrases:

1. The Yummy Pet Food Company is looking for 100 [consumers to] participate in an online survey of pet food buying habits, [and] we are willing to pay [each] participant $100 [for his or her time and trouble, but] we must begin [our survey] next Monday, [so,] if you are interested [in participating, please] e-mail us today, [sending your e-mail to the] attention [of Miss] Kitty Paas, kpaas@yummypfc.com, [in the marketing department.]

The following is one way to rewrite the message:

```
The Yummy Pet Food Company will pay $100 each to 100 partici-
pants in an online survey of pet-food buying habits. Our sur-
vey begins next Monday. If interested, e-mail Kitty Paas,
kpaas@yummypfc.com, today.
```

2. [This e-mail message has been written to alert all my clients of] my new e-mail address, ali@epolicyinstitute.com [which becomes] effective January 1, [and will make me available to respond to client needs more quickly, but if,] in the interim, [you need to reach me, please do not hesitate to] contact me [the good old-fashioned way,] via voicemail.

The following is one way to rewrite the message:

```
Effective January 1, my new e-mail address is
ali@epolicyinstitute.com. In the interim, contact me via
voicemail.
```

3. [Please] do not use the company's e-mail system for personal purposes, such as advertising [cars and other] items for sale, or notifying co-workers of the birth or wedding [of a child, and please remember that] this e-mail system is monitored by management, [and] we will not tolerate the use of off-color language, offensive jokes or other inappropriate material, [and] if the personal and inappropriate use of the corporate e-mail does not come to an end, we will be forced to take disciplinary action against [the] violators, [so knock it off.]

The following is one way to rewrite the message:

```
Do not use the company's e-mail system for personal reasons,
such as advertising sales or announcing births and weddings.
The e-mail system is monitored by management, who will not
tolerate the use of off-color language, offensive jokes or
other inappropriate material. Disciplinary action will be
taken against those making personal and/or inappropriate use
of the corporate e-mail system.
```

Rub Out the Paste (Page 39)

In the following sentences, power words are underlined, and brackets enclose the paste words:

1. [In the event that] the building loses power [and] the lights go off [during working hours, all] employees [are instructed to] remain seated [at their desks and] await the instructions [of the] department manager [who is assigned to supervise the activity of the department.]

    __16__ Number of Power Words   __28__ Number of Paste Words

The following is one way to rewrite the message:

```
If the lights go off during a power outage, remain seated and
await instructions from your department manager.
```

2. [I am sending this e-mail to all members of our association's board of directors to notify each and every member of the board of directors that] effective the first of the new year the board will meet [every] third Monday of each month [for the purpose of] discussing association business [matters.]

    __19__ Number of Power Words   __32__ Number of Paste Words

The following is one way to rewrite the message:

```
Effective January 1, the board will meet the third Monday of
each month to discuss association business.
```

3. [Per your e-mail directive of April 1: My understanding is that] <u>there is to be no more parking</u> [of] <u>employee cars in</u> [parking] <u>spots designated for visitors</u> [to the company, nor is there to be any further tolerance of healthy company workers parking their vehicles in spaces that have been designated for] <u>disabled persons.</u>

__16__ Number of Power Words   __38__ Number of Paste Words

The following is one way to rewrite the message:

```
Able-bodied employees are prohibited from parking in spaces
designated for visitors and/or disabled drivers.
```

Activate the Sentence (Page 43)

The following are possible ways to rewrite the sentences:

1. Memo recipients should e-mail responses to management by week's end.

2. During performance reviews, management will reward employees who adhere to company policy.

3. To curb employee theft at headquarters, the human resources director plans to assess job applicants' honesty.

Make It Gender Neutral (Page 46)

The following are possible ways to rewrite the sentences:

1. Employees who do not understand the department's e-mail policy should schedule a meeting with their supervisor.

2. The instructor must take the greatest care when explaining new concepts to students.

Part 4: Polishing Your Cybermanners

Assess the Flame (Page 55)

E-Mail Mistakes:

1. Angry tone.

2. Uppercase letters.

3. Exclamation points.

4. Misuse of "which."

5. Mistakenly believing his e-mail message would be read only by his intended audience.

Put Netiquette into Practice (Page 60-61)

Netiquette Errors:

1. Rude, hostile tone—what happened to the philosophy that the customer is always right?

2. Use of exclamation points.

3. Typos ("withing" and "upto").

4. No attempt to solve the customer's problem.

5. Use of insulting turn-off language.

6. The customer service rep is flaming the customer.

The following is an e-mail message you might use in the scenario involving slow delivery:

Dear Mrs. Katz:

On behalf of our entire organization, please accept my apologies for any confusion or frustration you may have experienced in the delivery of your new baby crib.

A check of our records confirms that your order for one deluxe baby crib (item #23456) was placed Monday, April 10. Two days later, on Wednesday, April 12, your order was processed and shipped via ground transportation. As noted in our online order confirmation form, shipping generally takes five business days. Your new crib should arrive at your delivery address by Wednesday, April 19.

Should you have any additional questions or concerns, be sure to reference customer code A123 in your e-mail message. I'm certain you and your little one will be pleased with your new crib. Thank you for your order.

Sincerely,

Francis Lambert
Customer Service Representative

Part 6: Managing E-Mail Overload

Devise Your Own E-Strategies (Page 83)

Personal E-Mail Management Action Steps:

1. Delete all spam and unsolicited messages. Do not take time to open or read them.

2. Sort business and personal messages. Forward personal messages from the office to my home computer. Handle personal e-mail on my own time.

3. Strive to write three-sentence e-mail messages whenever possible.

4. Limit the number of Listservs and electronic newsletters I subscribe to.

5. Stop e-mailing co-workers who are within walking and talking distance.

6. Copy only those readers with a legitimate need to read my message.

7. Assign my administrative professional the task of screening my incoming e-mail when I am on the road. Instruct my admin to delete all spam and unsolicited messages and forward personal correspondence to my home computer.

8. Remove my e-mail address from my business card to reduce spam and solicitations.

9. File e-mail newsletters and nonpressing messages for later review.

10. Turn off my e-mail pager in the evening and on weekends.

Organizational E-Mail Management Action Steps:

1. Develop and implement a company-wide e-mail policy that sets clear limits on personal e-mail.

2. Conduct company-wide e-mail management and e-policy compliance training.

3. Establish a document retention and deletion policy. Back it up with software that automatically deletes e-mail according to policy.

4. Install anti-spam software to stop offensive and unsolicited messages from entering our system.

5. Install content security and policy management software to monitor and control the messages employees transmit.

6. Reduce the size of employees' electronic mailboxes.

7. Ban the uploading and downloading of audio and video programs.

8. Instruct employees not to use e-mail for nonbusiness internal communications. Do not use e-mail to schedule lunch dates, plan after-work outings, and so on.

9. Ban the distribution of organization-wide, all-employee messages without authorization.

10. Conduct company-wide netiquette training.

A Glossary of E-Mail Terms

Acronym
A word formed from the first letters of a phrase's words. A common acronym used in e-mail is *LOL* for *laughing out loud.*

Address
The destination of an e-mail message.

Address Book
A collection of e-mail addresses.

Archiving
Storing old e-mail messages that warrant neither attention nor deletion.

Attachment
A computer file sent with an e-mail message. Examples: word processing documents, spreadsheets, databases, or graphics.

Backup
Saving data to an external source such as a disc or tape.

Bcc
Blind carbon copy

Cc
Carbon copy

CD-ROM
Acronym for compact disc read-only memory. Used for data storage.

Compression
File management technique that shrinks data for easy transportation and storage.

Cyberfraud
An illegal computer scam or con game.

Cybergrammar
The correct use of mechanics—grammar, punctuation, and spelling—in e-mail documents.

Cyberspace
The electronic environment in which people interact via computers.

Diskette/ Floppy Disk
A plastic or metallic object used to store computer data.

E-Mail
An electronic message transmitted between computers.

Electronic Correspondence
E-mail messages and attachments.

Electronic Jargon
Acronyms, abbreviations, and slang used and understood by a limited number of e-mail users.

Electronic Shorthand
A means for e-mail writers to express emotion. Not understood by all e-mail users. Example: <g> for grin.

Emoticons	Electronic symbols of emotion. Also called smileys.
Encryption	Scrambling of an e-mail message to ensure privacy. Once received, the message must be decoded by the recipient.
Filing	The organization of active messages and/or files.
Filters	An e-mail program feature that allows the user to sort incoming messages.
Flame	An angry or insulting e-mail message.
Folder	Related computer messages and/or documents that are stored together.
Forward	Retransmitting one e-mail message to a second user.
Group List	A roster of e-mail addresses.
Hidden Reader	An unintended e-mail reader, unknown to the writer.
Icon	A symbol on the computer screen that depicts an action or function. For example, a paper-clip icon could signify the attachment feature.
Inbox	The place where received e-mail messages are stored.
Internet	A worldwide collection of computer networks. Home to the World Wide Web. Always capitalized. Synonymous with the Net.
Intended Reader	The person(s) to whom the e-mail writer addresses and sends a message.
Intranet	A private computer network within an organization.
Modem	Hardware device connecting a computer and phone line.
Net	Synonymous with the Internet. A worldwide network of computers communicating in a common language via telephone lines or microwave links. Home of the World Wide Web.
Network Administrator	Person responsible for operating and maintaining a computer network.

Priority	Designates an e-mail message's importance—high, normal, or low priority. Lets readers know how quickly to open and act on a message.
Recipient	The receiver, or reader, of an e-mail message.
Reply	The response to an e-mail message.
Signature	A personal identifier at the end of an e-mail message. May include the writer's name, company name, and e-mail address.
Signature File	A predefined signature that can be inserted at the end of an e-mail message.
Smileys	Electronic symbols of emotion. Also called emoticons.
Snail Mail	Traditional method of mailing letters via the postal service.
Software	Computer programs such as e-mail or word processing.
Spam	Unsolicited junk mail delivered via e-mail.
Subject Line	Topic of an e-mail message.
Virus	An infectious computer bug. Symptoms range from mild distractions to major problems.
Word Wrap	Software feature that allows text to stay within defined margins. Eliminates the need to press *Enter* after each line.
World Wide Web	A global online information source of interconnected data. Also called the Web.

Recommended Reading

Andrus, Carol. *Fat-Free Writing*. Boston, MA: Thomson Learning/NETg, 2000.

Angell, David and Brent Heslop. *The Elements of E-mail Style: Communicate Effectively via Electronic Mail*. Reading, MA: Addison-Wesley Publishing Company, 1994.

Baker, Kim and Sunny Baker. *How to Say It Online: Everything You Need to Know to Master the New Language of Cyberspace*. Paramus, NJ: Prentice Hall Press, 2001.

Begley, Kathleen A., Ed.D. *Writing That Sells*. Boston, MA: Thomson Learning/ NETg, 2002.

Brock, Susan L. *Better Business Writing, Fourth Edition*. Boston, MA: Thomson Learning/NETg, 2002.

Flynn, Nancy. *The ePolicy Handbook: Designing and Implementing Effective E-Mail, Internet, and Software Policies*. NY: AMACOM Publishing, 2001.

Flynn, Nancy and Rudolph Kahn, Esq. *E-mail Rules: The Business Guide for Managing E-mail Policies, Security, Legal Issues, and Digital Communications*. NY: AMACOM Publishing, 2003.

Hale, Constance, Ed. *Wired Style: Principles of English Usage in the Digital Age*. San Francisco: HardWired, 1996.

Hartman, Diane, B. and Karen S. Nantz. *The 3 Rs of E-Mail: Risks, Rights, and Responsibilities*. Boston, MA: Thomson Learning/NETg, 1996.

Tarshis, Barry. *Grammar for Smart People*. NY: Pocket Books, 1992.

For additional information on e-mail writing, e-mail management, and e-policy development, visit the authors' Web site at www.epolicyinstitute.com.

About The ePolicy Institute™

The ePolicy Institute is dedicated to helping employers reduce electronic liabilities, while helping employees enhance their e-mail writing and e-mail management skills. Through the ePolicy Institute Speakers' Bureau, Executive Director and Author Nancy Flynn and other experienced trainers deliver keynote speeches and conduct e-mail writing, e-mail management, and e-policy seminars for corporations, associations, and government entities throughout North America and around the globe. Recognized as a leading source of expert information in the areas of e-mail writing, e-mail management, and e-policy development, The ePolicy Institute has been featured by *The Wall Street Journal, US News & World Report,* USAtoday.com, National Public Radio, *Woman's Day,* and other national and international media outlets. To book a consultation, speaking engagement, or media interview, visit www.epolicyinstitute.com or e-mail nancy@epolicyinstitute.com.

Customized workshops and keynote speeches based on the material presented in this book are available from The ePolicy Institute. Please contact Author and Executive Director Nancy Flynn for information:

Nancy Flynn, Executive Director
The ePolicy Institute
2300 Walhaven Court, Suite 100A
Columbus, OH 43220

Phone: 614-451-3200 Fax: 614-451-8726
E-mail: nancy@epolicyinstitute.com
Web site: www.epolicyinstitute.com

Notes

[1] Elizabeth Weinstein, "Help! I'm Drowning in E-Mail!" *The Wall Street Journal,* January 10, 2002. Article available online at www.epolicyinstitute.com.

[2] Elron Software, *1999 E-Mail Abuse Study.* Available online at www.elronsoftware.com.

[3] American Management Association. *US News & World Report,* ePolicy Institute *2001 Survey of Electronic Policies and Practices.* Survey results available at www.epolicyinstitute.com.

[4] Weinstein, "Help! I'm Drowning in E-Mail!"

[5] American Management Association, *2001 Survey of Electronic Policies and Practices.*

[6] Elron Software, *1999 E-Mail Abuse Study.*

[7] American Management Association, *2001 Survey of Electronic Policies and Practices.*

[8] T. Shawn Taylor, "E-Lessons," *Chicago Tribune,* February 14, 2001.

[9] American Management Association, *2001 Survey of Electronic Policies and Practices.*

[10] Barbara Carmen, "Fire Division Caught Peeking at Pornographic Sites on the Internet," *The Columbus Dispatch,* August 1, 1999.

[11] American Management Association, *2001 Survey of Electronic Policies and Practices.*

[12] Richard B. Schmitt, "The Cybersuit: How Computers Aided Lawyers in Diet-Pill Case," *The Wall Street Journal,* October 8, 1999.

[13] American Management Association, *2001 Survey of Electronic Policies and Practices.*

[14] NetPartners Internet Solutions, "1999 CSI/FBI Computer Crime and Security Survey," *Computer Security Issues & Trends* 5, no. 1 (Winter 1999): 7.

[15] American Management Association, *2001 Survey of Electronic Policies and Practices.*

[16] Ann Carrns, "Prying Times: Those Bawdy E-Mails Were Good for a Laugh Until the Ax Fell," *The Wall Street Journal,* February 4, 2000.

[17] L. Nicholson, "Oops, Wrong E-Mail Address List. A Dirty Joke Goes Global," *Philadelphia Inquirer,* May 8, 1999.

[18] Edward Wong, "A Stinging Office Memo Boomerangs," *The New York Times,* April 5, 2001.

[19] Elron Software, *1999 E-Mail Abuse Study.*

[20] Edward C. Baig, "Unlock the Secrets of Security for Your Laptop," *USA Today,* April 10, 2002.

[21] Excerpted from THE E-POLICY HANDBOOK, Copyright ©2001, Nancy L. Flynn. Published by AMACOM, a division of American Management Association International, New York, NY. Reprinted by permission of the publisher. All rights reserved. http://www.amacombooks.org.

[22] International Association of Administrative Professionals (IAAP) and The ePolicy Institute Online Poll, January 23, 2002. Survey results available at www.epolicyinstitute.com.

[23] Excerpted from THE E-POLICY HANDBOOK, Copyright ©2001, Nancy L. Flynn. Published by AMACOM, a division of American Management Association International, New York, NY. Reprinted by permission of the publisher. All rights reserved. http://www.amacombooks.org.

[24] Keith Naughton, "CyberSlacking," *Newsweek*, November 29, 1999, 65.

[25] Carrns, "Prying Times."

[26] American Management Association, *2001 Survey of Electronic Policies and Practices*.

[27] Wong, "A Stinging Office Memo Boomerangs."

[28] Ibid.

[29] American Management Association, *2001 Survey of Electronic Policies and Practices*.

[30] Weinstein, "Help! I'm Drowning in E-Mail!"

[31] Ibid.

[32] Darryl Haralson and Sam Ward, "Too Many E-Mails, Too Little Time," *USA Today Snapshots*®, March 12, 2001.

[33] Ibid.

[34] American Management Association, *2001 Survey of Electronic Policies and Practices*.

[35] Ibid.

[36] Excerpted from THE E-POLICY HANDBOOK, Copyright ©2001, Nancy L. Flynn. Published by AMACOM, a division of American Management Association International, New York, NY. Reprinted by permission of the publisher. All rights reserved. http://www.amacombooks.org.

VERN